The Wish-Fulfilling Wheel

The Practice of White Tara

This book is dedicated to His Holiness the seventeenth
Gyalwa Karmapa, Ogyen Trinley Dorje

The Wish-Fulfilling Wheel
The Practice of White Tara

by

The Venerable Khenpo
Karthar Rinpoche

compiled and edited by

Karma Sonam Drolma

Rinchen Publications
Kingston, New York USA

Published by
Rinchen, Inc.
20 John Street
Kingston, NY 12401
tel: (845) 331-5069
www.rinchen.com

ISBN 0-97145-542-2

Contents

The White Tara practice has played a vital role in the lives of such great masters as Atisha, Gampopa, and Jamgön Kongtrul the Great, and even in our own time it has been crucial in the lives of Kalu Rinpoche, Bokar Rinpoche, and Khenpo Karthar Rinpoche, among others. Moreover, it is upheld by all four schools of Tibetan Buddhism, each of which maintains a variation of the same original lineage. It is because so many people have attained realization and accomplished siddhi through this practice that Khenpo Karthar Rinpoche reminds us repeatedly in these teachings that "the practice of White Tara can bring you to complete awakening." Can there be a better recommendation?

In this book I have merged together all of Khenpo Karthar Rinpoche's teachings on the White Tara practice. Having done the practice in three-year retreat, I had always been enchanted with its simplicity and profundity, and was thrilled to have this opportunity to help make it more accessible to others. What I discovered as I went through the transcripts is a rare and unique teaching that can inspire experienced practitioners as well as beginners. These are authentic Kagyu lineage teachings that cannot fail to benefit whoever comes into contact with them.

Over the years, Rinpoche gave three different teachings on the White Tara practice. The transcript that forms the core of this book was the most extensive and detailed of the three, and comes from a month-long seminar he gave in 1986 at Karma Triyana Dharmachakra (KTD), the North American seat of His Holiness the Karmapa in Woodstock, New York. In 1990 he gave further teachings in conjunction with a White Tara retreat, also at KTD. The third comes from a weekend seminar he gave at Karma Thegsum Chöling (KTC) in Tampa, Florida, in the spring of 2002. Rinpoche based all of his teachings on Jamgön Kongtrul the Great's commentary on the White Tara practice and on the practice text written by Kunkhyen Tenpai Nyinje, the eighth Tai Situ Rinpoche.

During the 1986 teachings Rinpoche taught everything twice. As he went through the text, he would first give an initial explanation of some aspect of the practice. A few days later he would review that teaching and present his own commentary on it. Where it enhanced clarity, those two teachings have been merged together. However, sections in his commentary that might distract from the main line of thought have been appended as endnotes. That is also how I dealt with questions and answers from the original teaching sessions. If they enhanced clarity, they are merged into the teaching; if they covered topics not directly taught in the main teaching, they remain as questions and answers.

When merging the 1990 and 2002 teachings into the original edited transcript, I discovered to my astonishment that Rinpoche's 2002 teaching completely complemented his 1986 teaching in that details left out of one were present in the other, and vice versa. Both were illustrated with anecdotes, but they were different anecdotes, making the present book all the more rich and interesting. Also, although the 1990 teachings were short, they contained some precious jewels of insight and humor, which have found their way into this book. Altogether, the original three transcripts totaled 348 pages.

Tibetan and Sanskrit terms appear not as they are spelled in the original language but as they are normally pronounced. Those Tibetan and Sanskrit words and names that are now in common usage in English are not italicized, and their Tibetan or Sanskrit equivalents appear parenthetically in italics afterward. Words that are not widely used and therefore may be new vocabulary for many readers are italicized in both Tibetan and Sanskrit.

Appendices A and B contain the practice texts written by Situ Rinpoche and Jamgön Kongtrul Rinpoche. During the 2002 teaching in Florida, Khenpo Rinpoche went over the Situ Rinpoche text line-by-line, and I have adapted my translation of that text to his explanations. When this book was nearing completion, I asked Rinpoche to comment on the differences between these two practice texts. Each time I asked, however, he insisted that the two practices are identical. Since the texts themselves are not literally the same, what then could this mean? I came to the conclusion that he wants people to understand that the teachings he gave are equally applicable to both texts. Also, they are equally excellent practices. The blessings and fruit of doing both practices is the same. Neither one is better than the other. In other words, it is entirely up to you which one you do. Do whichever one you are most comfortable with, or alternate between the two.

From my own point of view, I have found the differences in the two texts to have great value. The Situ Rinpoche text is more formal and is a great aid in developing clarity, especially with regard to the offering visualizations. The Jamgön Kongtrul text has some lovely devotional language, and is a wonderful aid to enhance devotion. Also, although both practices are quite short, the Jamgön Kongtrul practice is the shortest, so it is a good option when time is limited .

If you are new to this practice, you might start with the Situ Rinpoche text because it is so helpful in developing the visualizations. Later, when you have become completely familiar with the visualizations, you can alternate the two practices or do whichever one you prefer. If you are doing a White Tara retreat with two or three meditation sessions a day, it is good to do the Situ Rinpoche practice in the first session and the Jamgön Kongtrul practice in a later session. In my three-year retreat, my retreat master had us alternate the two practices from the very beginning, and I still do that.

I am awed by Khenpo Rinpoche's great kindness and generosity in giving these rare and wonderful teachings. They are a treasure, and I pray with all my heart that my editorial efforts have made them more accessible and have not detracted from them in any way. I am very grateful to have been entrusted with this project, which has been so meaningful to do and has enhanced my own practice in the process. Any errors or omissions in the editing or translation are entirely my own, and I request the dakinis and protectors to be patient.

By the merit of everyone's efforts in having made this book possible, may Khenpo Rinpoche live for a very, very long time and continue to benefit numberless beings. He is truly a wish-fulfilling jewel. In that vein, I would like to call the reader's attention to Rinpoche's discussion in the book about using the White Tara practice to extend the lives of our teachers. I urge everyone who reads this book to take this seriously and to use this practice to pray for the long life of Rinpoche and the other great teachers of Tibetan Buddhism. With this in mind, and because it is not yet widely available, Rinpoche's new long-life prayer written by His Holiness in May 2002 is included as Appendix C.

I want to thank Khenpo Karthar Rinpoche for his patience in answering my questions. I also want to thank David McCarthy of Rinchen Publications for his unfailing help and support, as well as Kristin Van Anden, who has been a wonderful friend and inspiration. Her Sponsor's Dedication at the end of the book is testimony to her own personal and very deep connection to the White Tara practice. I am also deeply indebted to my husband, Lee Pritchard, because none of this would have been possible had it not been for his constant kindness and support. Last but not least, I wish to thank the three translators – Ngödup Tsering Burkhar, Chöjor Radha, and Lama Yeshe Gyamtso – for their fine translations, and Karma Triyana Dharmachakra in Woodstock, New York, and Karma Thegsum Chöling in Tampa, Florida, for their kindness in making the transcripts available.

May this book be of great benefit to all who read, touch, or even hear about it, and may numberless living beings find liberation through doing this practice.

Karma Sonam Drolma
January 2003

Acknowledgments

A book of this nature represents a great deal of dedicated work by a number of people, and I would like to express my deep appreciation for the fine job they have done. Having worked closely with each of them, I have been inspired by their altruism and commitment to the bodhisattva path.

First of all, we are indebted to Karma Sonam Drolma for her tireless and skillful work in making this book a reality. Not only did she do the extensive editing and organizing of the material, but she also translated the two practice texts of White Tara found in Appendices A and B. The completion of this book is an expression of her great devotion to Khenpo Karthar Rinpoche and her aspiration to make these teachings available to all.

We are also indebted to Louise Light, who did the complete book design, including the page layout, the interior graphic work, and the cover design. The end result is a testament to her prodigious professional skills and energy, not to mention her devotion, patience, and generosity over the many months it took to bring this project to completion.

I want to thank Kristin Van Anden, who made generous financial contributions to the production of the book and also contributed her literary expertise in the editing and review process. I also want to express my appreciation to Daia Gerson, who read the entire manuscript and made many valuable editorial suggestions.

My thanks as well to: Michael and Margaret Erlewine who provided the line art that appears in the book; to Lama Tsultrim who demonstrated the mudras; to Seichi Tsutsumi who took the photos of the mudras and provided the beautiful recent portraits of Rinpoche that appear on the back cover and in the book; and to Peter Van Deurzen who took the photo of the White Tara statue that appears on the cover. This particular statue was given to Khenpo Karthar Rinpoche as a birthday gift in the summer of 2002 by his students, together with many prayers for his long life. I would also like to extend my personal thanks to the translators of the source teachings for this text, Ngödup Burkhar and Lama Yeshe Gyamtso, for their tireless service to the Buddhadharma over the years.

Finally, I wish to express my gratitude and devotion to Khenpo Karthar Rinpoche, with the prayer that this book may be an appropriate reflection of the purity and profundity of his life and teachings and that it will bring about great benefit to countless beings.

David McCarthy
President, Rinchen Publications

Khenpo Karthar Rinpoche

Short Biography of Khenpo Karthar Rinpoche

The Venerable Khenpo Karthar Rinpoche was born to a nomadic family of modest means in Rabshu in the province of Kham in eastern Tibet at sunrise on the auspicious twenty-ninth day of the second month in the Year of the Wood Mouse (1924). He received the name Karma Tharchin, which was later shortened to Karthar.

Both of Rinpoche's parents were devoted Buddhist practitioners. His father was especially devoted to the bodhisattva Manjushri and constantly recited the Manjushri Sutra, often waking up in the morning with the words of the sutra on his lips. He taught Rinpoche to read and write at an early age. That made it possible for him to begin to study and memorize sacred Buddhist texts while he was still very young, and he did so with great enthusiasm.

As a child, Rinpoche always admired and wanted to become like his two older brothers, both of whom were ordained monks. Therefore when he was twelve years old, he left his home and entered the monastery, where he spent six years studying and practicing. When he was nineteen, Rinpoche went to Tsurphu Monastery, where for the first time he met His Holiness the sixteenth Karmapa, who was also nineteen. His Holiness was not yet old enough to give full ordination, so the following year Rinpoche received his Gelong vows from the eleventh Tai Situ Rinpoche at Palpung Monastery.

Shortly after becoming ordained, his two older brothers convinced him that he should do a solitary one-year Vairocana retreat. That retreat inspired a passion for practice in him that was to last his whole life. Therefore, shortly after completing this one-year retreat, Rinpoche entered a traditional three-year retreat. When he came out, he sold everything he owned in exchange for food, planning to remain in lifelong retreat in a cabin owned by his uncle.

A year after Rinpoche began his retreat there, however, the eighth Traleg Rinpoche summoned him out of retreat and asked him to study advanced teachings at a new shedra (university) he had founded at Thrangu Monastery. That shedra had been placed under the directorship of Khenpo Lodrö Rabsel. Khenpo Rabsel had received his training directly under the Shechen Gyaltsap Rinpoche, Pema Namdrol. (Khenpo Rabsel was the nephew of Pema Namdrol and the maternal uncle of Khenpo Gangshar.) Rinpoche entered this shedra, where he spent five years studying assiduously and maintaining strict discipline. He developed great faith in and devotion for his lama, Khenpo Rabsel. He was almost thirty years old when he completed his training there and received the title of Khenpo.

Rinpoche spent the following six years as a study attendant to Thrangu Rinpoche. These were happy and productive years, during which he and Thrangu Rinpoche traveled together and taught while pursuing their studies and having long discussions about the Dharma.

In 1958 the Chinese invaded eastern Tibet. Rinpoche's two older brothers were killed, but he and his younger brother, Lama Sönam Chödar, were able to escape in Thrangu Rinpoche's party, carrying with them whatever sacred objects and Dharma texts they could. Also in this party were Zuru Tulku Rinpoche and the three-year-old ninth Traleg Rinpoche. After months of travel and several mishaps, they finally reached Tsurphu Monastery in Tibet near Lhasa, where His Holiness the sixteenth Karmapa was staying. His Holiness was aware of the impending danger, and told them that they must leave immediately and go to Sikkim and India. He gave them five yaks and the necessary supplies, and by the end of March 1959 they reached the border between Tibet and Bhutan.

The first place they went after escaping from Tibet was a refugee camp established by His Holiness the Dalai Lama and His Holiness the Gyalwa Karmapa in Buxa, India, close to the border of Bhutan. This had previously been a prison camp for Indian political prisoners under the British Raj. About 1,500 monks of the four schools lived there, working tirelessly to reassemble the curricula of study of their respective lineages and to teach the Dharma in an effort to make sure that nothing would be lost. This was made possible through the kindness of the Indian and other governments, who provided the food and medicine to sustain them.

Because of the heat and harsh living conditions, however, illness began to spread like wildfire through the refugee camp, and by the eighth year of his residence there, Rinpoche himself had become extremely ill. In 1967 he appealed to His Holiness the Karmapa for permission to move to Sikkim, where he thought that the milder weather might help him recover. After a difficult and precarious journey, he reached Rumtek, where he stayed for the next five years, teaching the monks and ministering to the local Buddhist community. While there, his health remained uncertain, sometimes improving and sometimes getting worse. Finally, hoping that it would aid in his recovery, His Holiness sent him to Tilokpur, a nunnery in Himachel Pradesh founded by His Holiness and Ani Palmo, where he spent one year teaching the nuns. Because the water and other conditions were better there, his health began to improve and everything went very well. When he returned to Rumtek, however, his condition worsened again.

Hoping that he would find a cure there, His Holiness sent Rinpoche to Bhutan. He remained there for a few years, but his condition grew even worse, finally leading to a long hospital stay. The signs were getting more and more ominous, and it began to look as if Rinpoche might soon die. He asked His Holiness for permission to go into retreat to await his death. In response, His Holiness devised a plan in 1975 to send him to the United States so that he could get the medical care he needed. He also asked Rinpoche to be his representative and serve as the abbot of a new Karma Kagyu monastery yet to be built in North America.

When he arrived in the United States, Rinpoche was extremely weak and gaunt. With proper medical treatment, however, his health began to improve dramatically. During the first month he gained back all the weight he had lost during his long illness, and within a year he was restored to complete health. It seemed nothing short of miraculous. Years later, when he thanked His Holiness for saving his life, His Holiness told him that he would have died had he stayed in India.

When he first arrived in New York, Rinpoche only knew three people in the northeastern United States - Tenzin Chönyi, who had arrived in the United States the year before, and Lama Ganga and Yeshe Namdag, who had just arrived the week before. The first Dharma center they established was in New York City, and this eventually became known as Karma Thegsum Chöling (KTC). When His Holiness made his second United States tour in 1977, more KTC centers were established in Palo Alto (CA), Santa Cruz (CA), Columbus (OH), Albany (NY), and Cambridge (MA). In view of this growth, and in accord with His Holiness's wishes, a search was begun for a permanent site for His Holiness's North American headquarters. The Mead Mountain House was found in the mountains above the town of Woodstock, New York, in May 1978, and this became the monastery Karma Triyana Dharmachakra (KTD), with Rinpoche as its abbot.

In the years that followed, Rinpoche oversaw and traveled to a growing number of KTCs in North America, teaching extensively. In 1982 he traveled to South America and established two KTCs there as well. By the mid-1980s there were thirty-two affiliate centers in North and South America and three in Taiwan. Khenpo Karthar Rinpoche was now traveling to teach at all of them on an annual or semiannual basis, as well as giving teachings to a growing number of people at KTD.

During the summer of 1981 Rinpoche initiated a tradition of longer, more intensive teaching retreats at KTD. Until 1988, these consisted of month-long courses on such subjects as the Amitabha sadhana, the Uttara Tantra Shastra ("The Changeless Nature"), "Ground, Path, and Fruition," "View, Meditation, and Action," the Medicine Buddha practice, and the White Tara practice. In 1989 Rinpoche scaled back the length of his annual summer teachings to accommodate the growing number of students coming from afar. This was the beginning of the tradition of the ten-day teachings, which continue to this day at the time of the July Fourth holiday, often coinciding with the anniversary of Buddha Shakyamuni's first turning of the wheel of Dharma. Many of Khenpo Karthar Rinpoche's teachings have been published in both English and Chinese.

Rinpoche's other activities have been tireless as well, and include personally counseling a great variety of western and Chinese students new to the Buddhist path, as well as designing and overseeing the building and furnishing of KTD's three-year retreat center, Karme Ling, in Delhi, New York, and serving as its retreat master. The first three-year retreat in Delhi began in January 1993, followed by a second in November 1996, and a third in November 2000. Over the years Rinpoche has also found time to oversee and participate in all aspects of building, furnishing, and decorating the new monastery at KTD.

Introduction

Establishing a Firm Basis for Practice

To be meaningful and effective, the activities of listening to the Dharma, teaching it, and practicing it must be motivated by altruistic aspirations, which in Buddhism we call bodhicitta, or the mind of awakening. Without bodhicitta – that is, if a person's motivation is selfish – then no matter how much he or she studies or practices the Dharma, it cannot possibly serve as a remedy to the fixation on a self. Therefore it will not and cannot lead to the qualities we associate with spiritual practice. In fact, it is this very lack of bodhicitta itself that makes beings so unhappy. As long as beings are selfish – as long as they only want their own happiness – they will never achieve it. Nothing they do, not even spiritual practice, can possibly make them happy.

To develop altruistic motivation, we must begin by being empathetic. When we examine the situation carefully, it becomes apparent that there is no being anywhere who does not suffer, and there is no being anywhere who does not want to be free from suffering. There is also no being anywhere who does not want happiness. Unfortunately, there are almost no beings anywhere who actually get what they want.

Acknowledging this is the basis for developing loving-kindness, compassion, and bodhicitta.

In Tibetan Buddhism, love is defined as desiring the happiness of others. Compassion is defined as desiring that they have freedom from all forms of suffering. These two attitudes of love and compassion and the aspiration to free all beings from all suffering completely is what we call the mind of awakening, or bodhicitta. It is only through possessing this motivation that individuals in the past have ever gained accomplishment and enlightenment through their practice of Dharma. Moreover, it is only on the basis of this motivation that anyone will ever attain such a state in the future. Thus, whether or not spiritual practice produces qualities in you depends solely upon whether or not you possess the motivation of bodhicitta.

Space is infinite. It is utterly filled with all sorts of sentient beings. Each and every one of them wants to be happy. None of them wants to suffer. Unfortunately, most are ignorant about what constitutes the causes of happiness and the causes of suffering. Therefore, although they wish to be happy, they do not tend to engage in those actions that produce happiness. Likewise, although they do not wish to suffer, they engage in those actions that will cause them suffering in the future. Because of this ignorance and because of the actions produced by ignorance, sentient beings experience all of the many kinds of suffering that exist throughout the universe.

In order to get the most out of these teachings and this practice, we need sincerely and wholeheartedly to aspire to liberate all beings without exception from ignorance and from the suffering caused by ignorance. In addition, throughout our study and practice we must continually renew and strengthen this motivation.

Who Is Tara and What Does She Do?

Before we go into the details of the practice, you need to understand who Tara is, what she means, and why this particular form of Tara that we call the Wish-Fulfilling Wheel, or White Tara, is so particularly effective. Through knowing these things you will be able to develop enthusiasm for the practice. If you are enthusiastic about it, then you will do it. If you do it, you will reap its benefits. Therefore we will begin with a little overview and history of the practice to give you an idea of its significance and power.

Tara practice is extremely profound because the essential nature of Tara is primordial wisdom from beginningless time. We cannot say that at a particular historical point in time Tara appeared or became enlightened. Rather, through the power of skillful means she manifests as the play of the enlightened wisdom of all buddhas. Because all buddhas are born from the space of primordial wisdom, she is thought of as the source of all buddhas. That is why she is often referred to as the mother of all buddhas. If we analyze her name, we will understand her nature more clearly.

In Tibetan, we call her *Jetsunma Pakma Drolma. Jetsunma* means "venerable lady." The first syllable, *je*, implies nobility or a state of supremacy, and refers to the fact that she is the ultimate source of refuge from among all of the possible sources of refuge we might find in samsara and nirvana. The second syllable, *tsun*, means "noble" in the specific sense of "moral" or "true nobility." It implies that she is utterly stainless because she is free from all defects and stains of the mental afflictions, ignorance, and so forth. The syllable *ma* is a feminine ending, and is here translated as "lady."

The second part of her title, *Pakma*, is a Tibetan translation of the Sanskrit word *arya*, and means "elevated" or "exalted." She is exalted by her realization of the true nature of things. Because she possesses and indeed embodies ultimate realization, she is elevated above all defects coming from ignorance as well as all mundane defects. The second syllable of the word *Pakma* is *ma*, which means "mother." Because she has realized this ultimate nature and is indistinguishable from that nature, she can be regarded as a display of that nature. Therefore, according to the ultimate meaning, Tara is herself the dharmadhatu, the expanse that is the nature of all things without exception. Because she is not only someone who has realized this nature but is also that which must be realized for enlightenment to take place, she is the single object of realization of all buddhas. Therefore we refer to her as the mother of all buddhas.

Finally, her proper name is *Drolma* – or *Tara* in Sanskrit – which means "she who liberates." While ultimately she is that nature itself that is to be realized, she is not static. She is active. She liberates innumerable beings from all suffering and the causes of suffering through various means, including the display of various forms and even entire realms. Thus she is the embodiment of the ultimate nature of all things in a form that brings beings to liberation as a result of realizing it. The second syllable, *ma*, means that she is the feminine form of the enlightened ones. All the many appearances she manifests are in the female form. There is no manifestation of Tara that appears in the male form.

In our present world, the founder of buddhadharma is the precious Lord Buddha Shakyamuni. When we talk about his different kinds of teachings, they are generally divided into three basic classifications. They are vinaya, sutra, and tantra. Within tantra the Buddha taught various lineages of tantra. Among these are the *kriya, charya,* and *yoga* tantras.[1] *Kriya* is the lowest, *charya* is the middle, and *yoga* is the highest.

Within *yoga* tantra are three further classifications, known as father tantra, mother tantra, and union tantra.[2] Among the six million lines of tantra that the Buddha taught that belong to these three lineages, Tara falls into the mother tantra lineage.

The teachings on Tara were initially given by the Buddha pursuant to a request by the deity Hayagriva (*Tamdrin*). In the vajrayana, the Buddha often taught in response to specific requests for particular types of teachings. When someone made such a request, the Buddha would give those teachings and then make it that being's responsibility to guard or protect that particular collection of teachings. This first exposition made by the Buddha on Tara was known as *Ngön Jung Gyu,* which means "original," but also "fully complete." This latter definition refers to the fact that everything relating to Tara – the different visualizations, the mantras, and so on – are fully presented in it. It is "original" because of its original clarity.

Since ultimately Tara is the nature of the dharmadhatu itself, she has no single appearance and no single color. Nevertheless, since she is active in the realms and experiences of sentient beings, she is perceived in different ways. The *Ngön Jung Gyu* extensively explains the purity of the different forms of Tara, the different mantras of Tara, and the four activities of Tara. Twenty-one Taras are described, each one with a different form, color, and various aspects.

These different appearances of Tara are the same in essence. Yet in order to meet the different needs of beings, and as an expression of skillful means, Tara manifests in different forms. While she manifests in these different forms, however, there is no difference in essence. It is as if five people were looking into the same mirror. Five faces would appear, not because there are five mirrors but because there are five faces. The mirror, even though it is only one, has room for all five faces.

To give another analogy, the space of the sky cannot be differentiated. Sky is abstract and immaterial. Space is not form. It does not obstruct anything. To divide space, you would need obstruction, but that would be a contradiction in terms. Yet based on the layout of the world, people and countries create divisions of space, although there is no division of space that can be made practically. Based on what is under it, however, the United States can make a claim saying, "This is our sky," and another country can make a claim saying, "This is our sky." There is nothing there to divide the space, but based on individual circumstances there is a notion of that space as being "ours." It is not that the sky is different. In the same way, in accordance with the variety of beings and their needs, Tara manifests in different forms.

The nature of Tara is ultimate, but the world is relative. In the context of ultimate reality the nature of Tara is beyond concept and reference point. However, beings in relative existence can only relate to things on a relative level. The vehicle of the enlightened mind, the primordial essence, expresses itself in a skillful way so that beings' minds, which can only relate on a relative level, can understand. For this reason Tara appears in different forms and colors, although she is in essence beyond the concepts of color and form.

Generally speaking, White Tara is connected with longevity and the discovery of original wisdom. Yellow Tara is connected with the increase or expansion of merit, intelligence, and so forth. Red Tara is associated with attraction or magnetizing the entire world. Black Tara is associated with the forceful eradication of defects. Green Tara is considered to be the embodiment of all of these various forms of activity in one. In addition, Tara can manifest as inanimate objects. Anything that is beneficial and that can relieve suffering can be a manifestation of Tara's activity and compassion. Examples of this can be endless, and include such things as medicine, food, and water.

Quoting from the original *Ngön Jung Gyu*, the Buddha said, "The white one is to be used to save beings from untimely death," referring to the White Tara practice. Her special function is to promote long life. She has a wheel, like the wheel of Dharma, in the center of her heart. It has eight spokes, on which rest the syllables of the root mantra, and it is known as the Wish-Fulfilling Wheel. Ultimately White Tara accomplishes the liberation of beings from samsara, and relatively she liberates from the obstacles to a long life.

A Brief Overview of the Practice

White Tara was the main deity practice of many well-known Buddhist scholars and siddhas in India, who referred to it as "the one that embodies all," meaning that "doing one accomplishes all." Among the great teachers in India who took her as their main practice was Nagarjuna, who lived to be six hundred years old as a result of having accomplished the siddhi of longevity. Later, when the teachings came to Tibet, a great many realized beings there took Tara as their main yidam practice as well.

The earliest text describing this practice since the time of the Buddha was composed by a pundit in India, a great teacher and mahasiddha named Lobpön Ngagi Wangchug or Ngawang Drakpa (*Vagishvarakirti*). This great mahasiddha received the teachings on Tara passed down from the Buddha, and then White Tara actually manifested herself to him in person. This vision of Tara was as real as any two of us meeting personally face-to-face. Thus, he not only received the benefit of the teachings of the Buddha but personally received the transmission aspect of Tara. Subsequently, he completely realized and accomplished the practice, and it was passed down in a successive line, coming to Tibet in an unbroken lineage.

Ngawang Drakpa wrote a book called *The Prevention of Death*. This was a compendium of practices for increasing one's life span, including Amitayus, White Tara, and others. These were drawn not only from the Tara tantras but from many other tantras as well. Within that book is a chapter that gives the basic practice of White Tara and is the source for most of the traditions of White Tara practice that have come down to us today. A liturgy for the White Tara practice was then written by one of his disciples based upon what his guru had written in *The Prevention of Death*.

When talking about the lineage of Tara in Tibet, we talk about *ringyu* (the long or distant lineage) and *nyegyu* (the near or direct lineage). From the Buddha down to the present there was an unbroken lineage, and this is called the distant lineage. Later Ngagi Wangchug received the transmission from Tara directly, which further confirmed and intensified the lineage and is closer to our time. That is why it is called the *nyegyu*, or direct lineage.

The teachings and practices that came down from Ngagi Wangchug into Tibet developed into six lineages, and all possess great blessing. These six are all authentic lineages of the practice and therefore are all effective means for accomplishing the deity and reaping the benefits of that. They are the same in essence. The difference is only in the style of presentation and in the translations of those who brought the teachings to Tibet. This is like snow from a mountaintop. It melts and comes down in six different directions into six different valleys. These rivers flow in different directions and have different names. Their locations and appearances are different, but their essence is the same because they all come from the same snow. Similarly, there are six different teachings, yet in essence they are the same.

The six lineages are as follows: One was through Atisha and another was through Ngok Lotsawa Loden Sherab, a great translator. This latter lineage is known as *Ngokgyu*. Then another lineage developed through Bari Lotsawa, another translator. This is known as *Barigyu*. He was a contemporary of Milarepa. The fourth lineage was through Nakrinchen Lotsawa (*Vanaratra*), another translator, whose lineage was known as *Nakringyu*. The fifth is through Nyen Lotsawa Dharma Drak, and is known as the *Nyengyu*. The sixth originated in Tibet from a pupil of Atisha, whose name was Naljorpa, and is called *Naljorpa Gyu*.

White Tara is practiced by all the different schools of Tibetan Buddhism. With regard to our own lineage, the Dakpo Kagyu, it was passed down to us by Atisha, and has been done by all of the great practitioners of the lineage. This unbroken lineage is known as the Golden Rosary of Kagyu Masters.

Moreover, throughout the centuries since Atisha's appearance in Tibet in the eleventh century, many, many individuals have achieved both common and supreme attainment. "Common attainment" refers to the attainment of all forms of welfare and prosperity in this life, such as the pacification of illness and other mishaps, the increase of merit and wealth, the ability to have control over the events of one's life, the dispelling of obstacles, and so on. In the best cases, "supreme attainment" refers to the attainment in this very life of the same state as Tara herself – but it can also refer to accomplishment in two or three lifetimes. Once the state of Tara has been achieved, then for as long as cyclic existence persists, such a person will continue to be active in benefiting and liberating others.

Through this practice, innumerable individuals have dispelled or removed impediments that would otherwise have caused their deaths. This is significant because even though a person may have the karmic destiny to live for a long time, adventitious circumstances can still take their life in a moment. There are several ways to prevent this and protect oneself, and the practice of this form of Tara is considered foremost among them.

You will learn more about this as we look at the history of the lineage, because many members of this lineage have used this practice, as it says in Jamgön Kongtrul Lodrö Thaye's commentary on the practice, to "overcome the warfare of death" – that is, to overcome obstacles that would have caused untimely death. Some, when at the point of death, were able to double their life spans. Others increased their life spans by ten, fifteen, or twenty years, as we will see as the story goes on.

Keep in mind, however, that the purpose of this practice is not limited just to achieving the siddhi of long life or getting rid of obstacles to longevity. If it were limited just to that, it could be a problem for some people. If other complementary conditions are not present, long life can be painful. The scope of the practice goes far beyond that.

As explained earlier, the essential nature of Tara is primordial wisdom, which transcends dualistic extremes and reference point. It is the manifestation of the perfection of buddhahood. It is complete awakening. Therefore this practice alone is a complete method for accomplishing enlightenment and can lead to relative and ultimate siddhi.

The Benefits of White Tara Practice

Through study and practice of White Tara, we can accomplish four important aims. These are: (1) our own progress and ultimate attainment on the spiritual path; (2) the benefit of others; (3) upholding and serving the Dharma; and, very importantly, (4) accomplishing good health and long life for the great teachers of the Dharma so that they can benefit beings without obstruction.

For each of us, the most important thing in the world is to have a long and healthy life. It is like a precious jewel. It is the most important thing because no matter what we want to achieve, whether it be success in the ordinary world or success in the spiritual world through our practice of Dharma, a long and healthy life is essential. For example, a person who has a great deal of wealth as well as power, authority, and influence can have tremendous impact on or provide great benefit to himself and others. If his life is short, though, there is very little that he can do in spite of his endowments.

In this part of the world there are many different ways to promote a long and healthy life, such as medicines, diets, and methods of proper hygiene. Nevertheless, it is only through the Dharma that we can accomplish the siddhi[3] of long life and good health. This does not mean that external remedies (medicine, diet, hygiene) are not useful and good. It goes without saying that we need the proper external conditions that support and complement our lives. Optimal external conditions and remedies are only a beginning, however.

To reach the pinnacle of good health, quality of life, we need to develop our innate inner potential as well. The existence of a human being is dependent on his or her life force. It must be active. This depends not just on being nurtured and cared for physically (outwardly) but on our inner state as well. From among the various types of Dharma practice, White Tara is especially effective in realizing longevity on this level.

Long life and good health also enable us to benefit others. Our power and ability to benefit others depend on having a long life so that we can bring the greatest amount of benefit for the longest possible time. In addition, we can affect the lives of others. By practicing White Tara, we can clear away the obstacles in other people's lives that stand in the way of their experiences of long life and good health. In that way we can help them achieve longevity as well.

Finally, White Tara practice is an important tool for prolonging the lives of those who perform great benefit for beings. Through our practice we can help great beings in general, and particularly the enlightened masters of our own lineage who benefit beings on a vast scale, such as the Karmapa and the heart sons and great teachers who are well-known and travel everywhere to share the Dharma for the benefit of all.

In short, White Tara is symbolized by the wheel of the mantra in her heart and is known as *yishin korlo,* or Wish-Fulfilling Wheel. Since a wheel is beginningless and endless, it symbolizes that she fulfills all wishes without limitation of any kind. Through the virtue of this wheel and through the power of our genuine and wholesome intentions, not only longevity but each and every wholesome wish can be realized.

~

Student: Is it true that if you save life, the karmic result of that is to have a longer life yourself? How does that work, and how does it relate to White Tara practice?

Rinpoche: Living beings who have not yet achieved awakening are bound by confusion. Although they wish to prolong and improve their lives, much of what they do has the opposite effect. It actually leads to shorter lives because they do not understand what causes a long and healthy life. In their confusion they engage in unwholesome actions, such as killing and stealing, and this results in a shorter life.

What you have said is true. As much as you try to protect and save life, as the karmic result of that you will experience long life. Conversely, as much as you try to destroy life or help others to destroy the lives of beings, as a reflection of that karma you will experience a shorter life and many obstacles that lead to early death. On a mundane level, therefore, by protecting and saving life you can promote long life and help avert obstacles that lead to untimely death. In addition, for those who have taken a vow not to kill, even just the karma of having kept that commitment can lead to the experience of longer life.

To help avert obstacles and threats to the lives of others, it is good to save and protect life as much as possible, and to make prayers dedicating the merit of that to the benefit of all sentient beings, and particularly to the benefit of the person or persons you wish to help.

As I said earlier, the most effective way to promote long life and good health is the White Tara practice. Tara is a completely enlightened being who manifests in the female form so that with her motherly nature of compassion she can subdue the very hindrances that threaten life itself. Therefore, in our own situation the very best approach is to do both; that is, we should combine White Tara practice with whatever activities we can do to save and protect life.

Student: As beginning practitioners, can we practice White Tara right away, or is there a samaya that we have to complete ngöndro or something else first in order for our practice to be effective?

Rinpoche: Ideally, the preliminary practices of ngöndro should, as their name indicates, precede any other practice. Nonetheless, this practice has not been set up so that it can only be done by someone who has completed those preliminaries. Anyone who has received the empowerment, the reading transmission, and the instructions is free to do the practice. If you wish to do the practice intensively in a retreat, however, I strongly recommend that you begin by completing the preliminaries.

In any case, what is really needed for the practice to be effective is proper motivation and confidence. Proper motivation means that your motivation for doing the practice is grounded in compassion and bodhicitta. Confidence means trust in the validity of the practice, and it is best if this trust or confidence is directed toward both the deity and the lineage from which the practice comes.

Student: In the introduction you mentioned that White Tara can appear as medicine. In that case, it sounds like White Tara might be an excellent practice for health care providers. Can we use the practice in that setting?

Rinpoche: Definitely. I highly recommend this practice for health care professionals. In that case, you should attempt to combine your medical training, your altruistic motivation, and the power of the practice itself so that these three factors can come together in the healing activity. However, the danger at that point is that pride might arise, which would prevent the whole thing from working.

Student: You were talking about the different forms of Tara. I had always heard Yellow Tara described as increasing wealth, but I think you said increasing wisdom? Or did I hear that wrong?

Rinpoche: She increases all forms of qualities and virtue. It could be anything.

Student: If we have the karma to live for a certain number of years, how is it, then, that I read in some teachings of beings trying to take years away from us? And tonight I am learning about adding years to what I thought was a set karma.

Rinpoche: In general, what you are saying is true. Each of us has an allotted life span that is the result of our actions in previous lives. However, most people do not actually reach that full allotment in their lives, because obstacles or adventitious circumstances cause their premature death. It is a little bit like this: If you have an oil lamp and there is still oil left in the bottom of the lamp, then there is no inherent reason for the wick to burn out. But if a strong breeze comes, it can still put the lamp out, even though the fuel has not been used up. That is very much like adventitious circumstances or obstacles that can cause someone to die before the karma that would otherwise keep them in this life is used up. If you overcome or prevent the obstacles that will otherwise take your life, then you have the opportunity to complete your allotted life span.

But even beyond that, you can increase your allotted life span – because what we call karma is an obscuration of our basic nature. It is an imprint that is produced by the actions in which we have engaged. If the obscurations produced by our previous actions are to some extent removed, then the limitations they impose on our life span will also be removed. There are many examples of that. Perhaps the most renowned is Guru Padmasambhava, who by purifying all of his obscurations without exception has never died. He is still alive today.

There are many ways to approach longevity. Generally speaking, you work with the cause of life and death, which is the karma produced by your previous actions, and you attempt to purify that karma. You also work with conditions. This means working with physical means such as medicine and other things to provide the conditions for your longevity and health.

Student: When you say that Guru Rinpoche is alive today, do you mean in a physical form on this earth?

Rinpoche: When it is said that Guru Rinpoche is still alive, what is meant is that he has not abandoned the body he had when he was in Tibet. He still lives in that body. He never left a body anywhere. There are no remains of him. In terms of what kind of physical embodiment he has, it seems that he has the ability to vary this a little bit. To what extent the variation is occurring from his own point of view and to what extent from the point of view of the perceiver is very difficult to determine. The traditional explanation of where he is and what he is doing is as follows:

When he left Tibet in the ninth century, he left for a place that he referred to as "the island of rakshasas." A rakshasa is a type of being that is similar to a human being but not exactly the same species. Sometimes it is translated as "cannibal," but because they are a different species, it doesn't make much sense to call them that. Be that as it may, rakshasas eat humans. Guru Rinpoche left because he said that if he did not go there, they would take over this world and eat all of us up. From the point of view of the rakshasas, however, he appears as the ruler of all of the rakshasas. As to whether what he referred to as the island of rakshasas is part of this world or somewhere else is any-body's guess at this point.

The traditional explanation of the appearance of the king of the rakshasas is that he is an apparently fearsome individual with nine heads and so forth. In any case, the rak-shasas believe that Guru Rinpoche is their king and therefore they do whatever he says. In Tibet there are many stories throughout the centuries of tertons and other visionaries flying to Guru Rinpoche's realm, encountering him, and receiving his guid-ance. Visionaries, treasure finders, and others who have purified their karma and go to his realm in the midst of the island of the rakshasas, however, see him as Guru Rinpoche. There are also stories that he has continued to appear in Tibet occasionally throughout the centuries.

Student: Has he ever appeared outside Tibet?

Rinpoche: Definitely. He is not biased in any way. He said two things about his con-tinuing appearances in the conventional world. One thing he said that is often quoted is, "I will sleep blocking the door of anyone with faith in me." The other is, "There will be an emanation of Padmasambhava in the presence of each person with faith in me." He has promised that wherever there is supplication to him, he will appear in one way or another. It would not make any difference to him whether the people praying to him were Tibetans or someone else.

The Six Lineages & Their History

*A*s explained earlier, when the Tara teaching came to Tibet, six different lineages appeared, which continue unbroken to the present day. When we talk about an unbroken lineage, it does not simply mean that a person has the text for the practice of Tara, gives it to someone else for copying, they do likewise, and in this way the words remain intact just as they were when it was first passed down.

The expression "unbroken lineage" means that the meaning of the teachings is realized by the lama and is passed down to the student, who in turn experiences realization through the practice. The root lama is someone who gives teachings and instructions face-to-face and through whose guidance, instruction, and clarification the student practices and achieves realization. The lama and the student are different people, but their experience is the same experience. Only then is the student capable of holding that lineage and only then can that person properly pass it down to other students. This is how both the meaning and the realization of the teachings has been passed down, and this is the real meaning of the expression "unbroken lineage."

It is important to clarify the difference between a root and a lineage lama. The lineage lamas extend from the great Indian master Lobpön Ngagi Wangchug

(*Vagishvarakirti*) to the sixteenth Karmapa, and they all held the transmission in succession. However, just because they are lineage lamas does not mean they are your root gurus. Likewise, if someone is your root guru, that does not mean that he or she is a lineage holder. There is only one main lineage holder at any given time. Your root guru for a particular practice is the person through whose guidance you attain teaching and realization, and that may or may not be the main lineage holder.

Among the six lineages that developed in Tibet, the particular lineage that pertains to the short form of Tara practice we are working with is called *chöluk*. This is a tradition that comes from Lord Atisha. How did this particular lineage come to Atisha, who then passed it down to us? As explained before, there is the near lineage and a more distant lineage, called the direct and distant lineages. The distant lineage runs from the time of Buddha until this day. The direct lineage comes down to us from the great Indian mahasiddha Ngagi Wangchug, or Ngawang Drakpa. You will see his name in the lineage prayer.

Ngawang Drakpa had an actual encounter with a vision of Tara and from her received the complete collection of teachings. He became inseparable from Tara, and because of this complete realization he is considered to be the same as Tara. He passed the transmission down to his student, Serlingpa (*Suvarnadvipi*), a well-known mahasiddha, who then passed it down to Atisha (*Jowoje*). What sets the tradition of Atisha apart from the other five traditions in Tibet is that historically it was the first. It was the earliest form of White Tara practice propagated in Tibet and it was also the earliest effort to translate the White Tara teachings into Tibetan. Also, it is considered to be the most complete and extensive cycle of teachings on White Tara practice.

From among Atisha's many great Tibetan disciples, the lineage was passed to his foremost student, Dromtönpa, whose full name was Dromtönpa Gyalwa Jungney. Dromtönpa's realization was inseparable from that of Atisha.[4] He passed this realization on to a great Tibetan Buddhist master known as Geshe Chennga. The great master Chennga passed it on to a great bodhisattva and teacher named Drepa. Dromtönpa, Chennga, and Drepa belonged to the Kadampa lineage of Tibetan Buddhism.

Our first story about the White Tara lineage concerns the Kadampa teacher known as Geshe Drepa, who was the teacher of Gampopa. One night Geshe Drepa had a dream that the sun rose in the West and set in the East. He went to his teacher, Geshe Chennga, and told him about the dream. Geshe Chennga said, "That is a very bad dream. It is called 'the sun falling into the valley.' The sun is supposed to be in the sky, not in the valley. It is supposed to rise in the East and set in the West. It is not supposed to rise in the West and set in the East. It probably indicates that your vitality is being reversed. In short, I think it is a sign of death."

Then he went on, "However, we have profound methods in our lineage for preventing death, especially the practice of the Wish-Fulfilling Wheel, which is the name of White Tara. This is so profound that even if you have lost all of your limbs, it will still save your life." Saying that, he gave Geshe Drepa the teachings of White Tara.

Shortly afterward Geshe Drepa encountered a yogi called Tariwa of Lhadrup. This yogi was a siddha who was good at palmistry. He looked at Geshe Drepa's palm and said, "You have amazing karma with Dharma. Too bad you are only going to live for three years." When he heard that, Geshe Drepa put aside his study and decided, "Well, if I only have that long to live, I had better devote what little time I have left to intense Dharma practice – something that will really help me when I die." He decided to seek out an additional teacher, a realized master, to receive further instructions, so he approached another teacher called Geshe Lemapa. He told him about the dream and the palmistry reading, and this teacher said to him, "We have a method for avoiding death in our lineage – the practice of the Wish-Fulfilling Wheel," and he bestowed this teaching on him.

At that point, Geshe Drepa started to practice White Tara. He practiced intensively. After eleven months he had a vision in which he actually saw White Tara face-to-face. She said to him, "You will live to the age of sixty, and you will be able to benefit beings." When he reached the age of sixty he found that he had not yet completed all the work that he had started for the benefit of beings, so he again prayed to Tara. Again he had a vision of her and she said, "Have an image of me made and you will live another ten years." He had a painting created of White Tara, and he lived to be seventy.

At the age of seventy Geshe Drepa found he still had not finished the things he was doing for the benefit of others, so he prayed to Tara again and had yet another vision of her. She said, "Create another image of me and you will live another ten years." This time he had a statue cast in metal, and he lived to the age of eighty.

Though he had reached the age of eighty, he still had not finished everything he was trying to do. This time it was not even necessary to pray to Tara. She just appeared. She said, "All right. If you create another image of me, you will live for another fifteen years." Geshe Drepa had a mural of Tara painted on a wall in a temple near his residence, and he lived to the age of ninety-five.

A footnote needs to be added to this story. If his motivation had been selfish, Geshe Drepa would not have even seen Tara in the first place. The mere wish to stay alive is not enough. His wish for longevity was based upon his need to complete work for the benefit of others. Because his motivation was altruistic, his practice was very effective.

From Drepa the lineage was passed on to Gampopa, and thus it entered into the Kagyu lineage. Gampopa incorporated the Kadampa lineage into the Karma Kagyu mahamudra lineage, and since that time the Kadampa and the Kagyupa mahamudra lineages have been merged together, like the meeting of two rivers.

The White Tara practice played as important a role in Gampopa's life as it had in the life of Geshe Drepa. One day, when Gampopa was forty-one years old, he was practicing one-pointedly in an isolated retreat. While practicing, he had a vision of dakinis, who gave him a prophecy that he would die in three years. He continued to practice, moving from place to place and refining his realization.

At that time Geshe Drepa, who was already quite old, had become very famous as a teacher. He was renowned for having seen the face of Tara on many occasions. Gampopa decided to establish a Dharma connection with him. At this point Gampopa regarded his death as certain, so he was not motivated by the wish to lengthen his life. But because Geshe Drepa was a great teacher, he thought he should make a connection and receive some kind of teaching from him.

When he met him, Geshe Drepa looked at Gampopa and said, "You are an extraordinary and holy being. I am certain that there will be great benefit for others through your activity." In response to this, Gampopa said, "I don't have time to benefit beings. I have received a prophecy from the dakinis that I will die within three years." Great teachers always spend the early part of their lives perfecting their own training, study, and practice, and the later part of their lives turning the wheel of Dharma and benefiting others. Had he died in three years, he would not have had enough time to accomplish all of his dharmic activities.

Geshe Drepa seemed not the lest bit disturbed to hear this news. He said, "Don't worry. Even if they carry you off to the burial ground, we can get you back. Even if you see all sorts of signs and predictions of immanent death, we can fix it. I have the instructions to do it, and I will give them to you." Having said that, he gave the empowerment and practice of the Wish-Fulfilling Wheel to Gampopa. Gampopa practiced this and averted the obstacles that would otherwise have caused his early death. He lived to the age of eighty. His benefit for beings, as you may be aware, has been profound. The White Tara practice was passed down and upheld by the successive lineage because it had played such an important role in the life of Gampopa.

Gampopa passed the unbroken lineage to his foremost student, the first Karmapa, Dusum Khyenpa, whose realization was passed on to Drogön Rechen (also known as

Repa Chenpo).[5] Drogön Rechenpa, having fully accomplished realization, passed it to his foremost disciple, Pomdrakpa,[6] who passed it on to his foremost disciple, Karma Pakshi, the second Karmapa. Again in the same manner, he passed it to his foremost disciple, Orgyenpa,[7] who passed it on to Rangjung Dorje, the third Karmapa. Rangjung Dorje passed it to Yungtönpa,[8] who passed it on to Rolpai Dorje, the fourth Karmapa. He passed it to his foremost disciple, Khachö Wangpo, who was the second Shamarpa,[9] who then passed it on to the fifth Karmapa, Deshin Shekpa.

It is important to emphasize here, again, that this is an unbroken lineage of meaning and realization, not simply a package of knowledge passed down from one to the other. It is a lineage free of flaws because it is a transmission of meaning and realization and not simply intellectual knowledge. There is no difference between the teacher and the foremost student to whom the teaching is passed down. They are thought of as inseparable. They cannot be distinguished in terms of their depth of knowledge or realization.

Deshin Shekpa passed the transmission to Rigpe Raldri, who passed the transmission to the sixth Karmapa, Tongwa Dönden. From him it was passed to Bengar Jampal Zangpo, who was the author of the short Vajradhara prayer we do (*Dorje Chang Tungma*).[10] He passed it on to Goshri [Paljor Döndrup], who was the first Gyaltsap Rinpoche. Gyaltsap Rinpoche passed it on to the seventh Karmapa, Chödrak Gyamtso, who then passed it down to his disciple, Sangye Nyenpa Rinpoche.[11] He passed it to the eighth Karmapa, Mikyö Dorje, who passed it to his foremost student, Könchog Yenlak, the fifth Shamarpa.

Könchog Yenlak passed it on to Wangchug Dorje, the ninth Karmarpa, who passed it on to the sixth Shamarpa, Chökyi Wangchug. He in turn passed it on to Namdaktsen, who passed it on to the great siddha Karma Chagme.[12] He passed it to Dulmo [Chöje] Rinpoche, who passed it on to the eighth Shamarpa, Palchen Chökyi Döndrup. He passed it on to Tenpai Nyinje, the eighth Tai Situpa, who composed the brief daily practice of White Tara that we do. *[The full text of that practice appears in Appendix A. (Ed.)]* From him the lineage went to Dudul Dorje, the thirteenth Karmapa.

As you can see, three of the Karmapas (the tenth, eleventh, and twelfth) are not in this lineage. This was due to the fact that during the time of the tenth Karmapa there was a lot of political unrest in the country, making it impossible for him to receive the transmission. The eleventh and twelfth Karmapas did not receive it because they passed away at very young ages.[13] Instead, this particular lineage passed down through other great masters and then came to the thirteenth Karmapa.

The thirteenth Karmapa passed the transmission to Pema Nyinje Wangpo, the ninth Tai Situpa, who fully attained realization and passed it on to the fourteenth

Karmapa, Tekchog Dorje, who passed it on to his foremost disciple, Pema Garwang Tsal, which is the vajrayana name of Jamgön Kongtrul Lodrö Thaye, the first Jamgön Kongtrul. He was the original composer of the White Tara lineage prayer and also composed a second brief practice of White Tara that is done widely within the Kagyu lineage. *[The full text of this practice appears in Appendix B. (Ed.)]*

Jamgön Kongtrul then passed the lineage on to Khakhyab Dorje, the fifteenth Karmapa, who passed it on to Pema Wangchog Gyalpo, the eleventh Tai Situ Rinpoche. He passed it on to Khyentse Özer, who was one of the five "second Jamgön Kongtruls." He was the son of the fifteenth Karmapa and was based at Palpung. It was he who passed it to the sixteenth Karmapa, Rangjung Rigpe Dorje.

In this way the lineage has been maintained unbroken until the present day. We commonly compare it to pouring the entire contents of one full vase into another. Whatever is contained in the one vase is poured completely, every drop, into the other. In this way the unbroken lineage of the words, the meaning of the essential teachings and oral instructions, and the realization are passed down intact.

I myself received the empowerment, reading transmission, and instructions from the previous Traleg Rinpoche, Traleg Chökyi Nyima, who had received it from Duntrö Rinpoche, who was a disciple of Jamgön Kongtrul Lodrö Thaye.

~

Student: Could one say that any realized guru who is transmitting the lineage to a student is a lineage guru?

Rinpoche: During the time of each of these lineage holders, many hundreds of thousands of people experienced ripening through having received the transmission and doing the practice. However, it was only the foremost among them who was proclaimed and recognized as the lineage holder. Other lamas practicing within that lineage at the time were more like branches of the root lineage. A tree can have many branches, but there is only one main trunk. Without the trunk you can't have branches, but the branch is not the trunk.

In a way, each holder of the lineage is recognized by all the practitioners in that lineage at that time as a root guru, regardless of what their personal relationship may be. This is because the transmission lineage depends upon this lineage holder. Therefore, in an indirect way there is a root guru relationship. However, although everyone within the lineage recognizes the lineage holder as a root guru, as far as their own personal practice is concerned they may have a direct root guru relationship with another lama, having received direct personal instruction and guidance from him. Therefore your actual root guru is the one who has affected your life but is not necessarily the main holder of the lineage. He is like a branch of the trunk.

The Main Practice:
The Lineage Supplication

*T*he actual practice of White Tara begins with a supplication to the lamas of the lineage. There are several reasons for doing this. One reason is that all the members of this lineage had visions of White Tara, making their relationship with her and consequently their blessings very direct and powerful. Another reason is to strengthen confidence. We remind ourselves of the fact that these instructions come through an unbroken lineage – unbroken in the sense not only of the transmission of words, but also of the transmission of meaning.

The lineage supplication begins with the Sanskrit words NAMO GURU ARYA TARA YE. This means, "Homage to the Guru and Arya Tara." Then the first section of the lineage supplication goes through the names of the members of the lineage, which were discussed in the previous chapter. You may have noticed that from the time of Gampopa the lineage principally follows the mainstream lineage of the Karma Kagyu, known as the Golden Garland. The only departure from the main lineage occurs after the ninth Karmapa and the sixth Shamarpa. It reenters the mainstream lineage with the eighth Tai Situpa, Tenpai Nyinje, and continues down to the present with the main lineage all the way to the sixteenth Gyalwa Karmapa, Rigpe Dorje.

Then you recite, "To the Noble Lady who embodies all the root and lineage lamas and to those who hold the six traditions of her lineage of ripening, liberation, and dispensation I pray." While in emphasis this practice follows the lineage of Atisha, the supplication requests the blessings of the other five lineages as well, since all the lineages are the same in essence and all hold great blessing.

The lineage functions in two ways. The first is known in Tibetan as *min drol,* which means "ripening and liberation." This expression refers to the process that occurs when a beginner who receives instructions and guidance sincerely puts them into practice and gradually matures, finally achieving realization in one lifetime. An example of "ripening" is when a patient takes treatment and the treatment begins to have some effect. The pain gets less and the illness gradually diminishes. "Liberation" is when, at the end of treatment, the person becomes completely free of the illness. In the same way, this lineage of practice can lessen our confusion and so on, and finally lead us to liberation.

The second way that the lineage functions is known as dispensation, or *kabap* in Tibetan. Many of the great holders of the lineage had accomplished this practice in former lives, and had therefore participated in maintaining this unbroken lineage through reincarnating again and again as root and lineage lamas. Because they have already attained realization of the deity in previous lifetimes, when the teacher introduces the practice to them, there is an immediate experience of realization. *Kabap* refers to the awakening of the realization the student already has. Very little training is necessary other than some review.

Then you make the earnest prayer, "Bless that I perfect the stages of development, mantra, and completion, and accomplish the supreme vajra wisdom body of deathlessness." With this prayer you are aspiring that – with your defiled form with which you visualize, your defiled speech with which you recite the sacred mantra, and your defiled mind with which you practice the generation and completion stages of the practice – you realize a state beyond birth and death. This is the state of realization of Tara herself, the dharmakaya, the state of full awakening, where all obscurations have been removed and your actual state of being is the vajra wisdom body.

Finally you make the aspiration that having attained that state, "May I become inseparable from the Wish-Fulfilling Wheel who gives birth to all the victors, and spontaneously accomplish the two benefits." The two benefits or aims are (1) your own accomplishment of full awakening, victorious over all defilements; and (2) that having experienced awakening yourself, you can accomplish benefit for others by emanating whatever forms are necessary to fulfill the needs of beings. Another way of saying this is that the two benefits consist of the attainment of awakening in the form of the dhar-makaya for your own benefit, and the display of form bodies, the samboghakaya and nirmanakaya, for the benefit of others.

Most sadhanas are preceded by some form of lineage supplication. This is a very important part of the practice. When there is an unbroken lineage, there is something genuine about it. It is fresh and up-to-date. When you open yourself up in the presence of the lineage lamas, this can have tremendous power to help you accomplish the practice. Therefore it is very profound and practical. If you make the same prayers to some-one who has not received the transmission and is not a lineage holder, you will not experience the same benefit. It is like planting grains of sand. No matter how excellent the soil is, the grains of sand will not produce shoots. But when you sow seeds of real grain in the same soil, they will begin to grow. In that case you have the necessary con-ditions for a sprout to appear.

An earnest practitioner who enters into the practice, acknowledges the lineage lamas, and earnestly requests their blessings can take part in the goodness of the line-age because of the lamas' unconditional compassion and excellent qualities. Each line-age holder is inseparable from Tara. Though each has manifested the appearance of death to the eyes of worldly beings, in reality they are free from death. Therefore such a practitioner can experience the blessings of the lineage holders in a very noticeable way, and this is essential if they are to realize the meaning of the practice.

~

Student: How does the process of ripening and liberation work?

Rinpoche: Right now what we have is a physical body, with all its complications and shortcomings. We also have a fixation on this physical body as being something that is real and true. Through visualizing our body as the body of Tara, we can give rise to an experience that transcends that fixation. In this way we can give birth to a state beyond ordinary limitations. That is one aspect, which we call *kyerim*.

Another aspect is that presently our speech is full of shortcomings and defilements. The fruit of ordinary speech is most often harmful to ourselves and to others. For example, gossip and slander result in harm and the accumulation of habitual patterns for more harm in the future. We transcend and purify this kind of defilement and dis-torted speech through the use of mantra (*ngagrim*).

Finally, there is the stage of completion or perfection (*dzogrim*), where we experience the visualizations and mantras free of fixation and duality and rest in a state beyond reference point. Thus we begin with the visualization, and finally transcend even that, coming to rest in a nonconceptual state, the ultimate nature of reality. These are, in some sense, the stages. Right now we are beginning to grasp what the stages are, but this is not enough. We must actually realize the stages and become inseparable from Tara.

When we attain the state of Tara, we will attain the siddhi of deathlessness, but you will understand it better if I say it in a simpler way: We will have freedom over birth and death. It is deathlessness in that sense. Up to now, our experience of birth and death is a kind of birth and death over which we have no control. It is determined by circumstances outside ourselves, such as karma. We are subject to the force of decay. We are dependent upon others. However, for Tara or for anyone who has realized a state "beyond death," the experience of birth and death is not subject to outside conditions.

Once you attain such a state, the experience of birth and death will depend only on you. Whenever you want to die or manifest birth, you can. If you have freedom over birth and death, then dying and taking birth are not a problem. They are not painful. It is only when there is no freedom over it that you experience pain and suffering.

It may seem like a contradiction to say that all the lineage masters achieved the vajra body of deathlessness and then to say that all the lineage masters passed away. But there is no contradiction. To give you an example that may clarify this, let's say that someone has to clear a field where there are trees, rocks, grass, and so on. If he only has an ax, he can work on the trees, but if he tries to cut grass or boulders with the ax, it would be strange and difficult. Because of the different things he has to work on, he needs different tools. They look different and fulfill different functions. As far as the result is concerned, however, they are fulfilling the same purpose of clearing the field.

Likewise, different methods are necessary to work with different beings. The particular form or method that was effective for certain beings at a particular time is not necessarily going to be effective for beings of a different time, because the way their defilements manifest is different. Therefore enlightened beings appear in various ways simply to get things done. They manifest for the benefit of others. In the analogy, the person who is working on the field is like the mind of Tara, which is beyond death. The tools he uses to clear the field are the manifestations of the enlightened beings. The different tools look different but serve the same purpose.

Through understanding how to practice and through actually doing the practice we can realize the essence of Tara. When we have realized the essence of Tara, then we will be inseparable from Tara and the lineage holders. Having achieved such realization, we will be free from the sufferings of birth, sickness, old age, and death. Moreover, we will be free from habitual and emotional tendencies such as the three poisons (attachment, hatred, and ignorance). These poisons or their offshoots are the causes of all of our confusion and suffering.

It is essential that we realize Tara because we cannot benefit others in our present state of confusion. When we are completely free from these limitations, however, we will be able to benefit others without limitations, difficulties, or sufferings, just like the great bodhisattvas who work continuously to benefit beings. Then, for as long as cyclic existence is not empty of suffering, the activity of benefiting others will continue unceasingly and spontaneously.

The Main Practice: Going for Refuge

*A*fter the lineage supplication, we begin by taking refuge in the perfect enlightened objects of refuge. In addition, we generate the enlightened mind, which means turning our minds to the proper motivation, or bodhicitta. These two must occur at the beginning of any practice of the mahayana or vajrayana in order for it to be authentic. Doing a practice without them is like walking, but going in the wrong direction.

At present, we are like someone who has a serious illness. Our minds are afflicted by habitual patterns and defilements that cause suffering now and will cause suffering in the future. As such, what do we need to do and to whom should we go for help and refuge?

In general, taking refuge is something familiar to us. Throughout our lives we are continually taking refuge of some sort. For example, when we were children, we turned to our parents as the source of refuge, help, and protection whenever there was danger, discomfort, unhappiness, or the desire for comfort and security. Later as adults we depend upon other people and objects as a kind of refuge – a possible shelter from which we imagine we receive an element of protection or security.

Some people even perceive some aspect of nature, such as a big mountain, a big tree, or an ocean as having the power of being a sanctuary, and think of these objects as refuge. Others, who need someone to look up to, honor their ancestors, hoping that their ancestors will somehow hear them and be there for them when they need protection or security. Still others turn to a well-known person in the world, a popular personality known for having done something constructive or good on a large scale. Thus the notion of going for refuge is not particularly new to us.

Even in our own experience, however, we can see that the objects commonly taken to be a refuge have shortcomings, because it is obvious that these objects cannot ultimately bring anyone freedom from suffering and confusion. Not only that, it is clear that through relying on them we often encounter more problems than benefit. Though it may sometimes seem like there is some benefit at first, perhaps because of our own hopes, in the long run more harm than benefit occurs because of the shortcomings of these objects.

This is because these objects themselves are subject to the confusions and limitations of cyclic existence. They are not liberated from their own self-clinging and ignorance, so how can they help free us of ours? If we suffer because of our harmful habitual tendencies and we look for inspiration to objects of refuge who themselves manifest these same patterns, that could add to the problem rather than solve it. Using the analogy of the sick person again, if we approach a so-called physician who has heard of diseases and treatment but is unaware of what treatment affects what disease or what causes a disease, it would not be helpful.

Thus it is evident that regardless of how much other knowledge they may possess, most beings have not found proper objects of refuge. They have not developed the wisdom to understand what a true object of refuge is because they lack proper guidance. They also lack the intelligence to see beyond their own coarse and neurotic relative reality.

What are the characteristics of a true object of refuge? First, to be genuine, an object of refuge itself must be free from the confusion and harmful habitual tendencies that cause suffering. This is true because if we wish to become free of the real, ultimate causes of our suffering and shortcomings, we must relate to objects of refuge that are free from such causes of suffering themselves. Only then can they be a useful inspiration, aid, and example. Second, a genuine object of refuge must be fully committed to liberating others from the causes of suffering. This demonstrates that they have true compassion and kindness for others.

When we consider what the characteristics of a genuine object of refuge must be, we begin to understand that the only true object of refuge is Buddha. As has been explained on many occasions, the word for buddha in Tibetan is *sang gye. Sang* literally means "purified," and here means completely purified of all defilements, and therefore refers to freedom from all habitual and emotional tendencies. *Gye* means "to flower" or "to expand," and here refers to the flowering of complete wisdom and knowledge – the completely awakened mind. Thus the Buddha is one who is free of all defilements and endowed with perfect and complete knowledge and qualities.[14]

Because the Buddha is free of confusion and suffering, he can lead others to the same state. This is the greatest possible benefit, without mistake or shortcoming. Therefore the Buddha is the only true object of refuge. When taking refuge, we acknowledge the Buddha for what he is, and make the aspiration to follow his example. We need his guidance and inspiration in order to do so. To obtain that inspiration and guidance we take refuge in him. Therefore, not only do we find Buddha inspiring but we take refuge in him. We are doing something about it. This means we have a very special vision about our lives. We are going to try to fulfill its ultimate potential.

Since the Buddha is our example of ultimate sanity, to follow the same path that he followed is the way to attain freedom. We must remember that all the buddhas were at some point in the past ordinary beings like ourselves. Like us, they had suffering and habitual patterns that caused suffering. Through applying proper remedies and not giving up the path to liberation through confusion, they ultimately obtained complete liberation, knowledge, and wisdom. It is something they developed and earned. Therefore this is something we can do too, because it has been done by ordinary people. We can follow their good examples. This is very practical, as evinced by their accomplishments.

Having taken refuge in the Buddha, we must sincerely acknowledge the methods that lead to the experience of buddhahood. In the same way as the buddhas have done, we need to apply the proper remedies if we are to attain freedom from suffering and confusion. That is why we take refuge in the Dharma. Dharma in Tibetan is *chö*. It refers to the teachings of the Buddha – the path or methods he taught that lead to perfect liberation.[15]

Therefore, not only do we admire the Buddha – but we wish to strive to experience the same state the Buddha experienced. The enlightenment of the Buddha is evidence that this is the true path. This is a pragmatic approach. Taking refuge in the Dharma in this way means acknowledging the path and making a commitment to the path. This is the true meaning of taking refuge in the Dharma. If you do not acknowledge the path and commit to the path, then you have not taken refuge in the Dharma.[16] It is similar to the situation in which a sick person takes refuge in the treatment that is prescribed by his doctor. To become cured of the sickness in a practical way, the patient must relate to the treatment as well as to the physician.

In the mahayana form of refuge, we take refuge from this moment until we have achieved complete awakening – that is, until we have realized whatever the Buddha realized. In other words, we take refuge until we have realized the complete teachings of the Dharma. Taking refuge like this is an intelligent and pragmatic approach to attaining freedom from suffering. It is not just a vague idea without practical importance. We take refuge with full confidence that there is something in our lives that needs to be taken care of and that this is the proper approach.

It has been over 2,500 years since the Buddha applied these methods, and the inspiration of his physical presence is no longer available to us. How shall we go about applying the Dharma to our lives? For this, our relationship to the Sangha, or *gendun* in Tibetan, is indispensable. From the time of Buddha until this present day, those who have held and preserved the unbroken lineage of his teachings and experience are the Sangha. If they did not introduce us to the stages of the path, we would have no chance to practice the genuine Dharma. Therefore we take refuge in the Sangha.

The Sangha is the assemblage of spiritual friends. It is described as supreme among all gatherings and as the basis for the accumulation of merit. The teachings have come down to us in an unbroken lineage due to the efforts of the great lineage holders, who have taken upon themselves the responsibility to see that these teachings are preserved and made available to us. Having done this, they are the source of the greatest possible accumulation of merit. Such Sangha are indispensable spiritual friends, so we take refuge in them.

Let's look at this from another perspective. When the Buddha lived, we were not fortunate enough to meet with him. Because of our own ignorance and confusion, we did not have the karma to be born at the time and place where the Buddha taught. Still, even though the Buddha passed away, his teachings are still available because the Sangha has preserved them in an unbroken lineage. Nevertheless, we do not have enough virtue to apply the teachings through our own effort alone. We could not practice properly and fully without the help of spiritual friends. It is only because of their kindness that we are able to begin to learn and understand the teachings, and eventually to gain realization through the practices.

Clearly, the Sangha is indispensable. They make liberation from suffering and confusion a reality. They are an essential part of the journey. They show us how to do it. They are the spiritual authorities who are both examples and inspiration. They hold the lineage of the teachings. Taking refuge in the Sangha is acknowledging their indispensability and their role in this important journey, and realizing that it is only because of the kindness of the Sangha that one can experience the benefits of the teachings. Again, this is very practical.

~

Student: Do buddha emanations know who they are? How does one recognize them? Do they recognize each other?

Rinpoche: They know what they are and who they are, but it is very difficult for us to recognize an emanation of a buddha and to distinguish them from anyone else because there is almost no limit to what form they might take or what they might be doing. The only thing we can guarantee about them is that they will be a source of either immediate or ultimate benefit for others, or both. They will not be engaged in something that is harmful to others. Aside from that very general statement, they could appear as just about anyone or anything and do just about anything, so there is no way for us to recognize them. However, emanations of buddhas do recognize themselves and they can also recognize other emanations of buddhas.

The Main Practice:
Generating Bodhicitta

*W*ithout a genuine, impartial commitment to the well-being of others, buddhahood cannot be achieved. Bodhicitta acts like a boat that carries us on our journey to buddhahood. Through developing perfect kindness and compassion toward others, the buddhas all attained enlightenment, free from suffering and confusion, endowed with perfect knowledge, wisdom, and the ability to benefit beings on a vast scale. This attitude is the most important aspect of our practice if we wish to attain enlightenment. Therefore it is essential that we generate the enlightened aspiration of bodhicitta.

Our aspiration should not be limited. We must generate the attitude, aspiration, and commitment to accomplish the liberation of all beings without exception – not just from some sufferings and pains but from suffering altogether.

To be able to actually benefit beings, we need to have accumulated a great deal of merit. The best way of accumulating merit is through making wholesome aspirations. Therefore we dedicate the merit of all our virtuous actions – be it through the practice of generosity, moral conduct, or any of the other paramitas, or the merit of hearing, contemplating, and practicing the teachings, as well as whatever other merit we have accumulated in the past, present, and future – to the realization of enlightened mind.

The sooner we achieve enlightenment, the sooner we can benefit beings on a vast scale. Until then, the greater we have developed, the more benefit we can accomplish. Therefore there is an urgency to this, and in this way we pray to attain enlightenment quickly.

As a means of cultivating the pure enlightened mind of bodhicitta, we recite and contemplate the four immeasurables, or *tse may shi* in Tibetan. Through contemplating the four immeasurables, we come to understand the nature of beings, what they are going through, what they need, and what should be accepted and what should be abandoned. This helps us to train our minds to have the proper aspirations.

The first immeasurable is "May all beings have happiness and the causes of happiness." This is what we wish for all beings, not limiting our wish just to the people of one country or group, nor to a particular gender, nor to humans alone. We make this wish for all sentient beings in whatever form they appear, wherever they appear – for all sentient beings who have feelings and consciousness and are capable of feeling pain and suffering.

Ordinarily, what beings think of as happiness can be a source of future suffering. This is not the kind of happiness we wish for them. All states of genuine happiness arise from previous states of virtue and virtuous actions. This is what we wish for them because it leads to present and future happiness and ultimately to the great happiness of buddhahood itself. Training the mind like this develops loving-kindness, or *jampa* in Tibetan.

The second immeasurable is limitless compassion, or *nyingje* in Tibetan. We pray, "May all beings be free from suffering and the causes of suffering." We are praying that all beings without exception become free from whatever physical, mental, and emotional sufferings they have, including the suffering of being deprived of what they need or want, the great sufferings of those in the lower realms, and so on.

We wish them to be free not only of their present suffering but also of the causes of all future suffering. Thus, since states of unvirtue and unvirtuous actions are the causes of suffering, we are wishing that beings be free from all the habitual tendencies and obscurations that cause all the different varieties of suffering. We earnestly aspire that they all be liberated right now. This is not just an idea. It is a commitment.

When we make the aspiration in this way, it is immeasurable compassion because we make this aspiration for all sentient beings, who are limitless in number. Another reason it is immeasurable is because it is not limited to just one type of suffering, such as the suffering of heat only, or pain only. It includes every suffering that any being can experience. Likewise, it includes any and every cause of suffering – whatever obscurations, habitual patterns, and confusion there are. In all these ways it is immeasurable.

The third immeasurable is known as immeasurable joy, or *gawa* in Tibetan. This is expressed by the line, "May they never be without that genuine happiness that is free from all suffering." This immeasurable is the result of the first two. Having happiness and its causes and being free of suffering and its causes is the experience of the ultimate happiness of buddhahood. This state of awakening is beyond all suffering. It is the mind of perfect joy. This happiness is not like ordinary worldly happiness, which is not complete. It is total joy – perfect happiness – not subject to any form of change, limitation, or suffering. We sincerely long for all beings to experience such a state, and the thought of their achieving it is a cause of great joy for us.

The fourth immeasurable in Tibetan is *tang nyom*. Literally, this means "to even out," but it is more accurately translated as "impartiality." We pray, "May all sentient beings abide in that great impartiality that is free from attachment and aversion to those near and far." Presently there are those we like and those we dislike. There is a constant experience of attachment and aversion, and this is a cause for more and more suffering. Only when we abide in a state of impartiality will we be free from suffering and the causes of suffering.

In this fourth immeasurable, not only do we restate our own impartiality in directing the three previous aspirations equally toward all beings but we make the aspiration that all beings themselves cultivate such a state of perfect impartiality. It is important to note that impartiality here is not a state of impartial apathy or impassivity. To make that clear, it is called "great impartiality," which means impartial compassion.

In this way we generate bodhicitta and train our minds through contemplation of the four immeasurables. As we progress, however, it is not enough to just train our minds with the tools of the four immeasurables. Just as one mute person cannot talk to another mute person verbally, in the same way one person who is deeply caught in the afflictions cannot liberate others. Therefore we must make a realistic effort to attain freedom from all of our defilements and limitations so that, once we are free, we will have the ability to benefit others. This practice is a skillful means for accomplishing that end. Now, with the sound basis of generating the four immeasurables, we enter into the practice of White Tara, the Wish-Fulfilling Wheel.

The Main Practice:
The Development Stage (Kyerim)

Self-Visualization

*A*lthough they are basically the same in essence, vajrayana practices begin differently than do the practices of the mahayana and hinayana. In hinayana and mahayana practices we are working with what is available and relating to the raw materials. In that process we are practicing and working with what our minds can immediately relate to on a relative level. However in vajrayana, rather than working with a cause that will ultimately bring a certain result, the focus is on fruition, and it is from this perspective that we approach our practice. This is like someone who is working with a light fixture. He has a light bulb, wires, screws, and so on. While these are the tools he is working with, he still has in mind a clear picture of what the result will be when it is all put together. In the same way, to properly engage in White Tara practice, we need to make appropriate preparations. We prepare our minds and our view of the phenomenal world in such a way that they can accommodate Tara.

Tara is the mother of all buddhas. She is the perfect wisdom that gives birth to enlightenment. Therefore the practice begins with the mantra OM SHUNYATA JNANA BEDZRA SOBHAWA EMAKO HAM. With this mantra we meditate on emptiness as a preparation for generating ourselves as the deity. To understand the importance of this, it is necessary to understand the problem that it is remedying. The problem is that we mistake all things that we experience or perceive as being real from their own side. We think of them as having an inherent existence separate from our perception of them. It is through mistaking all things to be real that we generate mental afflictions. On the basis of mental afflictions we engage in afflicted actions, and on the basis of that we come to suffer in what we know as the six realms of cyclic existence. Therefore the fundamental problem that we need to remedy is the mistaken misapprehension of things as real. The remedy for this is recollection of their true nature, which is emptiness.

Though it is very challenging in the beginning to relate to this, it is absolutely necessary that we do so. From a practical standpoint, contemplation of emptiness at the beginning of a visualization practice creates the space in your mind that allows the visualization to develop. This is necessary because if you try to practice the visualization within the state of reification of appearance, you will not be able to imagine it because the visualized image will be obstructed by your perception of things in the external world as real.

Nevertheless, it is important to remember that the obstructions you are removing are not caused by the appearance of solidity itself but by your mind's concept of solidity. Therefore in contemplating emptiness in the beginning you are not attempting to alter the appearance of things but to relinquish your habitual conceptualization of things based on their mode of appearance as solid, substantial, inherently existent, and so forth.

To the degree to which you let go of these concepts – that is, to the degree to which your fixation or obsession with appearances diminishes – to that degree there will be a corresponding amount of space in your mind allowing easy visualization. Therefore this initial contemplation of emptiness is as necessary for the generation stage visualizations as it is for the completion stage practices that come later.

The *shunyata* mantra purifies the environment and mental misconceptions. It involves dissolution of defiled projections of mind from the point of view that all things lack true existence because they are impermanent and interdependent. With the word *shunyata*, meaning "emptiness," we acknowledge the essential emptiness of all phenomena.[17] Keep in mind that emptiness in the Buddhist teachings is emptiness beyond dualistic extremes, beyond reference point. It is not nihilism.

Through developing this pure outlook, wisdom (*jñana*) manifests. This is ultimate awareness free of dualism. The inseparable union of unchanging or indestructible (*bedzra*, sometimes pronounced *benza*)[18] wisdom and emptiness is the nature (*sobhawa*) of all phenomena, free of contradiction. The words *emako ham* say that "I am resting" in this inseparability of indestructible wisdom and emptiness. With this mantra, we rest in the nonconceptual fundamental nature of mind – clarity and emptiness. Awareness of the nature of all phenomena as the indestructible union of wisdom and emptiness is both the beginning point and the fruition we are working toward.

Putting it all together, the literal translation of the *shunyata* mantra is: "All things and I are the embodiment of that indestructible wisdom that is emptiness." Remember, though, that this mantra is not some kind of magic spell that causes things to disappear or dissolve into a state of emptiness. Emptiness is not something you are trying to turn things into. It is what they already are. So the purpose of the mantra is not to transform things but merely to help you recollect the actual nature of things as they always have been.

After saying the mantra, rest in the experience of emptiness. Resting in emptiness, however, is not thinking, "Things are empty." Resting in emptiness is simply resting without any kind of mental concept. Rest simply, without fixating on anything whatsoever. This means not fixating on objects of apprehension or their characteristics and not fixating on that which apprehends them – the mind. Resting in that way for however long you can is the first stage of the practice. It can be done for an instant, or it can be done for a long time. Either is fine.

After resting in emptiness, you then recollect that while all things are empty – without true or inherent existence – this is not to say that they are nothing. As a sign of that, from the state of inseparable emptiness and wisdom and as an expression of that emptiness, the essence of mind[19] arises as the sound HUNG. The syllable HUNG is to be thought of here as a sound. That is, it is not a visible syllable. You can think of it as something like thunder. This sound fills all of space, and from this comes an encircling protective vajra fence and tent. In this way, the mind is giving birth to the encircling vajra fence and tent, which is therefore the appearance of mind and is nothing other than mind. This part of the practice is done to remind yourself that while we think of emptiness as a negation, as nothing, in fact what we mean by it is that the nature of all things without exception is the unity of appearance and emptiness.

The circle of protection is white and dome-shaped. Everything is constructed of white vajras that resemble white crystal. Below is a vajra ground – indestructible and impenetrable. It is flat, with an enormous crossed vajra lying flat in the center. All of the spaces within the double vajra and between the four parts of it are filled with smaller vajras, and then with even smaller and smaller vajras, so that it is completely solid and there is no space in between. Nothing could ever get in or get through it. That is what forms the ground.

Rising up from the perimeter of this vajra ground, which is circular, is a vajra wall in three stages. The first stage consists of many vajras standing upright, forming a fence of vajras. Above them is a fence of vajras lying flat, and above them is another level of vajras standing upright. As with the ground, all the holes are filled in with smaller and smaller vajras, leaving no gaps. Not even the slightest wind can penetrate it. It is total protection.

upright vajra

Coming off the top of this wall and forming a roof or dome overhead is another enormous double vajra, the prongs of which are bent downward. From the inside it is somewhat concave or domelike, and from the outside it is convex and domelike. As before, all the spaces within that and between the parts of that are filled with smaller vajras and yet smaller vajras so that there is no space anywhere. It is impenetrable.

crossed vajra

The domed ceiling is adorned with a vajra canopy, which hangs below it, somewhat like a lowered ceiling, and it is shaped like the spherical shelter on top of a tent. This is composed entirely of vajras as well. In the center of the actual roof above the canopy is a vajra pointing upward. Half of this vajra sticks out above the roof, and half comes down into the space under the roof. From its upper point comes a lamplike flame.

The circle of protection is visualized as composed of vajras in order to bring the recollection of indestructibility. The shape of a vajra represents indestructibility – something that is so hard, so tough, that it cannot be disturbed. It cannot be cut, destroyed, or moved. It is stable, permanent, and immeasurably tough and hard. While visualizing the vajras as looking like the scepters we use, remember that this is symbolic. Indestructibility here does not mean something physical that is indestructible. It means the indestructibility of the basic nature, which is so strong, so immovable, and so indestructible that no force in nature or anywhere else could ever disturb it to even the slightest degree.

This vajra tent and fence are encircled by a blazing fire of the five colors. If you were to look at it from the outside, you would see a hemisphere of multicolored fire. The flames move in a circular, clockwise direction. It is an impenetrable environment, free of obstacles. It is inconceivable, vast, and spacious.

It is important to know the details of the circle of protection because most vajrayana sadhana practices have a vajra protection circle and they are all similar. If you know the visualization for one sadhana, it will help you to practice the other sadhanas in the future as well.

In the center of the circle of protection appears the syllable DRUNG. This is the seed syllable of Buddha Vairocana (*Nampar Nangdze*). This is transformed into the palace of the deity. It is made of what is described as "watermoon crystal." It is not really crystal because it is beyond materiality, but it is described this way to help us grasp how it appears. Watermoon crystal is a naturally occurring form of crystal that reflects like the light of the moon. It is transparent and hard, somewhat like clear glass, but with a slight whiteness or moonlight-like gleam. As used here, it is a metaphor. "Moon" implies that it is cool, crisp, clear, white, and bright; "water crystal" expresses its clarity, transparency, and freedom from defects.

DRUNG

The term "palace" in Tibetan is *shelyekang*. This is a potent expression referring to something beyond our ordinary concepts about what a palace is. Literally, the expression means immeasurable, inconceivable, or inestimable mansion. It is like a celestial palace. It is not a material palace. The mind generates it instantly. It is not constructed like an ordinary building. Instead, spontaneously, in a moment, it appears.[20] It is beyond concepts of size or substantial materiality. With the exception of the difference in the colors, it is the same as the palace in the Medicine Buddha practice.

The palace has four sides and four doors facing the cardinal directions, each with a large doorway, and emerging from each doorway is a portico – a covered entrance. It has one large chamber and is square. Above the walls is a space, and above this is an ornamental four-sided pagoda-shaped roof with an elaborate cornice that goes around the perimeter of the building and extends slightly out beyond it. The roof is supported by four crossbeams, which rest on the walls above the door frames, and four octagonal pillars, which are situated around the central part of the floor. The pillars are made from precious gems, and are white in color. Garlands of precious gems and pearls are strung from the roof in the space above the walls, and they have small bells hanging down from them. The entire palace is brilliantly luminous, both inside and outside.

The four sides of the palace symbolize the four immeasurables: love, compassion, joy, and impartiality. The four doors facing the four cardinal directions signify fulfillment of the four enlightened activities: pacification, enrichment, magnetizing, and subduing. The space between the top of the walls and the roof symbolizes emptiness. The garlands of precious gems strung down from the roof in that empty space symbolize that emptiness does not mean that there is nothing. There is wisdom in emptiness. The bells hanging down symbolize that within emptiness the Dharma is being taught effortlessly.

In the center of the palace you visualize a white PAM. This becomes a fully open white lotus on its stalk. The stalk starts in the very center of the palace. The lotus is full-

pam

grown, fresh, and huge. It is often said to have a thousand petals, but it is not necessary to count them. Just think of it as fully blooming, with many petals. Above the center of the lotus you visualize a white syllable AH. This syllable melts into light and becomes a full-moon disk free of stains and impurities. A full-moon disk is a stainless disk of white light – a full and perfect circle of white light that rests immediately on top of or above the center of the lotus flower.

AH

On top of this seat, the essence of your mind appears as the white letter TAM, which is the seed syllable of Tara herself. You will remember that you previously dissolved everything into emptiness in the sense that you contemplated the emptiness of all things. Now, while not departing from that recollection, you nevertheless focus on your mind as being present within the midst of the visualization, now in the form of the seed syllable. With this process of visualization we have formed the basis for the visualization of ourselves as the actual deity.

TAM

The TAM is now transformed into a white utpala flower, and resting on the center of that flower is a white TAM. From the utpala flower and especially from the white syllable TAM in its center, immeasurable light rays radiate up and out, making vast clouds of excellent offerings to the buddhas and bodhisattvas in all directions. Having made these offerings, all buddhas and bodhisattvas are pleased in body, speech, and mind, and you accumulate great merit. The light returns back with their blessings to the syllable TAM.

Then light rays radiate out and downward toward all beings of the six realms, bringing a sense of clarity, like bright lamplight in a dark place. The light purifies their obscurations, frees them from suffering, and establishes them in a state of liberation.[21] The light again returns to its source, and dissolves back into the TAM. At that instant the TAM and utpala flower are transformed into yourself as White Tara, seated on the moon above the center of the lotus. Your visualization should be free from solidity. It is the inseparability of emptiness, clarity, and wisdom.

In describing the appearance of White Tara, it is important to note that all of her physical attributes are a skillful expression of vajrayana methods. Deity practice is one of the most profound methods because the forms indicate the meaning or essence. The form of a deity is not just a form but a vehicle through which the meaning is skillfully expressed.

Tara's body is the color of white crystal. It is cool, crisp, stainless, clear, and free from flaws. It glows and radiates lights of the five colors, which represent the five wis-

doms. This does not mean that from one part of her comes one color and from another place another color. From each part of her, as though from each pore of her skin, emerge countless rays of white, yellow, red, blue, and green light. It is something like the way a crystal, when the sun shines on it, will produce a rainbow or spectrum.

She is very beautiful and completely feminine. She is not only perfect in form but also graceful in expression and engaging in appearance. There is something about her that is utterly captivating. She appears to emanate great

White Tara

affection and love. Her face bears the expression of great peace that is not impassive. It is an expression of utter tranquillity that is also very kind – something like the way people tend to smile at children with affection. Thus she combines tranquillity and a loving disposition in both appearance and expression.

Traditionally, to help us imagine Tara from our own perspective, it is taught that she is like a young virgin of sixteen without defects. But a better way of describing it is to say that she is beyond description. Words fail to describe to the conceptual mind the beauty of such a form. We can only say that any being who might have the good fortune to see her would, no matter how acute their suffering or obstacles, be liberated just at the sight of her. The sight of her would be overwhelming. Whatever was would be no more. It would be forgotten – gone. Even if the immediately preceding moment had been one of tremendous pain or suffering, at just the sight of her we would forget it all.

This description is intended to help you understand her appearance, but at the same time to help free you of your conceptual limitations. If, on the contrary, we were to describe the form in minute detail, or if we were to rely on an artist's concept of what is beautiful, we would become entangled in the limitations of conceptual mind. Tara's beauty transcends that. Regardless of what concepts anyone has, she is perceived to be beautiful. If you actually experience Tara, then you will definitely become liberated from suffering. Keep in mind, however, that only people who have become free of defilements can see such a vision. It is only because they have purified all defilements and accumulated inexhaustible merit that they have the maturity to experience that vision.

One thing that is slightly unusual about Tara's appearance is that she has more eyes than most of us. Most of us have two. She has seven. She has the two usual ones, and in addition she has a third eye in her forehead, which is vertical. Furthermore, she has an eye in the palm of each hand and an eye in the center of the sole of each foot. These are called the seven eyes of wisdom.

I have heard an explanation of the meaning of this, but have never seen it verified in commentaries. It is said that these seven eyes represent the fact that she gazes compassionately on the beings in the seven situations, and brings them to liberation. The eyes in the soles of her feet represent the fact that she gazes compassionately on the beings in the two lowest realms – the hell and preta realms. With the eyes in the palms of her hands she gazes compassionately upon animals and asuras. With the two usual eyes she gazes compassionately upon humans and gods, and with the third eye in her forehead she gazes compassionately upon beings who have achieved cessation or nirvana – the shravaka and pratyekabuddha arhats who have not yet attained the full awakening of buddhahood.

Elsewhere it has been explained that the three eyes on her face represent the inseparability of the three kayas, which are primordially pure and not subject to defilement. The four eyes on her palms and the soles of her feet symbolize the four immeasurables – immeasurable loving-kindness, immeasurable compassion, immeasurable joy, and immeasurable impartiality.

Her right hand is in the gesture of supreme generosity, with the face of the palm open outward, resting upon her right knee. This gesture symbolizes supreme giving. She gives whatever beings need and do not have. It represents the gift of skillful means, the gift of inspiration, the gift of the qualities of realization, and the gift of the various noble activities, which are expressions of completely awakened mind and which beings need so much and do not have.

At her heart, between the thumb and ring finger of her left hand, she holds the stem of a white utpala flower, which blossoms beside her left ear. The fact that she is holding the stem of the flower with the thumb and ring finger pressed together represents the inseparability of phenomena and their nature. The stem is held at the heart level to signify that her mind is never separate from the dharmakaya, and to indicate the inseparability of the dharmakaya and form kayas.[22]

The three upright fingers symbolize that the Three Jewels – the Buddha, Dharma, and Sangha – benefit beings in whatever way is necessary. They appear not only as the Buddha, Dharma, and Sangha but also in any form necessary to accomplish the benefit of beings – even such ordinary things as food, water, or insects. Thus she manifests the three kayas for all beings in whatever forms meet their needs.

No matter what form she manifests, however, she is never susceptible to the defilements of samsara. This freedom is symbolized by the white utpala flower forever blossoming at her left ear. Even though this flower grows out of the earth, it is free of the dirt from which it comes. This symbolizes her freedom from samsara and the defilements.

This utpala flower actually has three blossoms. The center one is fully blossomed; the one above has not only blossomed but appears to have aged; and the one below is a bud about to open. These three blossoms signify that there is no time during which Tara does not benefit beings. The older flower represents the times of the past buddhas, the central flower represents the time of the present buddhas, and the unopened bud represents the times of the future buddhas.[23] The Situ Rinpoche practice text says that the flower has a hundred petals. This is not to be taken literally. It is just a metaphor to indicate that it has many petals.

The fact that these three blooms all come off of one stem and that she holds this with that particular gesture to her heart means that while we would normally think of the buddhas of the past, present, and future as different or at least as distinct, ultimately they are of the same nature in Tara.

Tara is adorned with a great deal of finely crafted and elegant jewelry. It is composed of various forms of jewels and precious materials, but predominant among the jewels are pearls. Her crown is a head ornament of the Buddha family, which has five separate diadems made of various jewels. You have doubtless seen these in pictures of peaceful deities. She also has earrings of precious jewels. She has three types of necklaces; one short, one medium, and one long. The short one is a kind of choker. The medium one hangs to just above the breast. The long one hangs to just above the navel. Her arms are adorned above the elbows and at the wrists with arm bands and bangles, and her legs with anklets. She has an ornamental belt encircling her waist that is like gold intertwined with elegant fabric, with little bells hanging in a weblike formation from it. It is adorned with precious stones, semiprecious stones, and precious metals. Altogether there are eight different kinds of precious jewelry.

Normally people wear jewels to exhibit their wealth or in the hope of enhancing their appearance. But Tara has no such concepts. The precious jewelry she wears is an expression of her enlightened qualities and activities. The four activities of enlightened beings are pacifying, enriching, magnetizing, and subduing. Principally, Tara appears in peaceful form and benefits beings through various pacifying activities. To signify this, she wears mainly pearls. The other jewels symbolize the activities of enriching and magnetizing. She is also wearing garlands of flowers, especially in the tiara on her head and the longest necklace. These are like the flowers you could find only in the god realms.

Tara is adorned with five silk garments. Not all of them are mentioned in the text, but you should know about them. The first one is like a sash that ties the crown on. The second one partially covers her hair and goes down the back. It is one piece, and is tied to the knot of the hair. Third, her upper garment is a loose blouse of white silk, and is very fine and light, like the silk of the god realms. It is a garment not to be found in our world. Fourth, she wears a lower garment of flowing silk of different colors, like a rainbow, underneath which is an underskirt of blue, the lower edge of which is just visible below the edge of her skirt. The fifth is a belt like lace, on top of which is the jeweled belt described above. Around the waist it is quite wide. From that a long lace sash is hanging down to her feet (like tapestry lace). It has fringe and strings of beads strung with little bells. The lace belt is studded with three jewels at the point where it interlaces above where the sash begins.

All those deities who appear in the samboghakaya form have the same number of adornments, and each will predominantly display more of whatever type of adornment expresses their main type of activity. In this case, the white pearls express Tara's main activity of pacification. As far as the number of adornments is concerned, however, there is no difference between Tara and other deities. Altogether, there are always thirteen. That is why Tara has eight kinds of precious jewels and five garments. According to vajrayana, the stages of enlightenment are thirteen, with the thirteenth being the highest and representing the final state of complete awakening.

There are two explanations of how Tara's hair is tied. Originally, it was described as being tied at the back of her head. That is how she appeared in the traditional paintings in India. However, when the teachings came to Tibet, it changed in some lineages. That is why it is sometimes described and shown as being tied on the top of her head.

This particular practice is true to the original. Therefore the text literally says "bound in back." Half of her hair is coiled in a knot behind her head, and the rest of it flows freely down her back, especially to either side. The hair coiled in a bun represents that in their ultimate meaning all things are coiled into or partake of the single nature of the dharmakaya. This ultimate meaning can manifest in different forms in the relative world, but the ultimate meaning is one. Once ultimate realization is attained, there is no cessation – the enlightened mind displays uninterrupted enlightened activity. That is symbolized by the other half of her hair going down and hanging freely. The hair falling freely to her right and left means that while not departing from that nature or the realization of that nature, she manifests the samboghakaya and nirmanakaya for the benefit of beings.

Her hair is deep dark black, very fine and silky. Each strand is perfect and untangled. This is symbolic of indestructibility. Unlike other colors, black cannot be changed by other colors. No obstacle or intrusion of any kind can change or cause degeneration or damage. This symbolizes that the ultimate meaning that is realized cannot be changed, destroyed, or stained. The symbolic meaning is important. I mention this because these days talented artists like to make all kinds of changes and may make Tara with brown hair instead of black. This is a misunderstanding. We are not relating to human hair here. There is a reason why the hair appears in this particular way.

She is seated with her legs fully crossed in perfect vajra posture in the center of a moon disk, and she has a full moon as her backrest. What is the meaning of these symbols? When we originally described Tara, we said she is the essence of dharmakaya, beyond measure, time, and concept. In whatever form Tara appears she is inseparable from dharmakaya, and that inseparability is indestructible. This is symbolized by the vajra posture.

The moon behind her back also expresses indestructibility, but indestructibility in another sense. Because she is completely enlightened, she always has the quality of freshness – like the moon giving light. It is cool, fresh, and peaceful. Accordingly, her activities always have this quality of peacefulness, gentleness, and coolness. That quality of her manifestation is indestructible insofar as it does not just happen sometimes and not at other times. It happens all the time – immeasurably and inexhaustibly.

It is good to keep in mind that when we say she has a moon as a backrest, that does not literally mean a backrest like the back of a chair. It is referred to that way because when it is depicted, it looks like it is behind her. But in fact, the moon is like a halo. A halo is not a flat thing. It is almost like a globe of brilliant light that emanates from her. Though it might look like it is behind her, in a sense it is all around her.

In this way you visualize the complete appearance of yourself as Tara in every detail. Though Tara appears, she is empty and luminous, like a rainbow. Inside the empty, hollow enclosure of her body, in the center of her forehead is a luminous white syllable OM. At her throat is a red syllable AH, and a little below her heart center is a blue syllable HUNG. In the Buddhist teachings, it is said that OM is the essence of the form of all enlightened beings. AH is the essence of the speech of all enlightened beings. HUNG is the essence of the mind of all enlightened beings. In the midst of your body, at the level of your heart you visualize a white lotus, and on top of that a moon, a disk of white light. Standing upright on top of that is a white syllable TAM.

white OM

red AH

It is important to always keep in mind that each aspect of the form of the deity symbolizes a particular important meaning. Each introduces the ultimate meaning or expresses aspects of ultimate meaning. Therefore the deity is the meaning. A deity is not like a form composed of organs, bones, flesh, and so on. It is not subject to limitation and destructibility. It is a form that transcends these and communicates meaning.

blue HUNG

In addition, you cannot do justice to the practice if you relate to the form with yourself as the reference point; for example, when you have a certain feeling and think that the deity has this same feeling. Instead, you should relate to it as a form beyond concept – as an embodiment of ultimate enlightenment. You can then approach that state yourself. Because you arise as the deity from the state of emptiness, this form is like a mirror that brilliantly reflects the luminous wisdom and blessings of the actual deity herself.

In this way the vajrayana teachings are very profound and deep. In some sense that is why they are difficult, because we are not working with what exists relatively but with what does not exist on a relative plane. Through this, the relativity of our ordinary situation is exaggerated to the point that we actually begin to perceive its relative nature. This is accomplished by training ourselves to relate to things in a different way than our conceptual minds are accustomed.

In the hinayana, mahayana, and sutras on the other hand, we use what is available in a way that we are used to on a relative level. To give you an example of the difference between the tantra and the sutra teachings, think of a field of sand that has a precious jewel in it. The sutra approach to finding the jewel is to clear away all the sand. After you have gotten rid of all the sand, you will have the jewel. However, the vajrayana approach is to leave the field of sand as it is, but to go find the jewel. Either you get it or you do not get it. You get it in a more direct way. But if you go for it with hopes and expectations and you fail to get it, it could be a very devastating and frustrating experience.

Accomplishment of the Deity

Since at this point you may have the thought that your visualization of Tara is simply an act of imagination, it is helpful to invite the actual deity Tara, the wisdom being herself. To do so, you visualize white, red, and blue lights emanating from the three syllables and the TAM, invoking the actual wisdom deity from the pure realms, her natural place of residence. Ultimately, you would have to say that since she is the nature of all things, she has no particular place of residence. Nevertheless, in terms of how she is perceived, she abides in the realm of the Potala – the pure realm of the Bodhisattva Avalokiteshvara.

When you recite the mantra BEDZRA SAMADZA and do the appropriate mudra, Tara herself appears above you in the space in front, surrounded by her retinue.

BEDZRA SAMADZA means, "Through the power of your commitment for the benefit of beings, I ask you to come here." The wisdom being Tara looks exactly like the self-visualized deity. You, as the visualized deity, are the *samayasattva* or commitment deity (in Tibetan, the *damtsig sempa*). This refers to your commitment to visualize yourself as the deity. The wisdom deity is the *jñanasattva* (in Tibetan, the *yeshe sempa*).

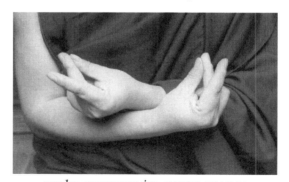

mudra accompanying BEDZRA SAMADZA

From your heart as the *damtsig sempa* eight offering goddesses are emanated. As you recite the offering mantras, each goddess makes her particular offering to the *yeshe sempa* in front – the offerings of drinking water, bathing water, flowers, incense, light, perfumed water, food, and music. When you are making these offerings, your body, speech, and mind should be fully involved. With your mouth you are saying the mantra for each offering: OM BEDZRA ARGHAM SOHA, and so on. With your hands you do the mudra for making each offering. With your mind you approach it as described below.

First, white light is emanated out from the seed syllable TAM in your heart, and from this a white offering goddess appears. She is graceful and beautiful and adorned

drinking water offering mudra ~ ARGHAM

with many beautiful jewels. She emanates many thousands just like herself. All of these make offerings of drinking water to the wisdom deity Tara and her retinue in front of you, and she is very pleased. It is important to know the meaning of these offerings. Although Tara has no need for water and would not be disappointed if we did not offer it, we do this because it brings great benefit to sentient beings. Because of the virtue of having sincerely made this offering and having pleased the *yeshe sempa*, the suffering of thirst of all beings is quenched. Especially, it quenches the thirst of beings who are suffering from thirst for the nectar of Dharma. Their thirst is quenched and satisfied, and they are liberated. You make this offering with the aspiration that all beings' thirst be completely satisfied, both on a relative and on an ultimate level. With the mantra OM BEDZRA ARGHAM SOHA, you hold your hands in a mudra like a cup being offered with great respect.

Next, the syllable TAM in your heart radiates dark red light, and from that a dark red offering goddess manifests. This red offering goddess also emanates many thou-

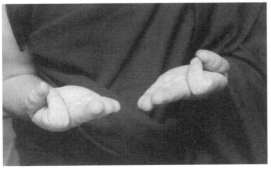

bathing water mudra ~ PADYAM

sands just like herself. Each of these offering goddesses holds a basinlike container made of precious jewels in her hands, which is filled with clean, pure, scented water for washing. Traditionally, this is used to wash the feet of the deity. In this way, you offer cleansing. Again, it is not that Tara has need of such a gift. Instead, we make this offering because of the result it accomplishes. Through the merit of having sincerely made such an offering, whatever undesirable and harmful stains all beings have are purified. Especially, it purifies their inner mental defilements, including the various kinds of habitual tendencies. You make the offering with the aspiration that all beings have such purification. As in the first offering, your body, speech, and mind are involved. With your speech you are saying the second mantra, OM BEDZRA PADYAM SOHA. Your hands are in the appropriate mudra, and the offering is being made with the mind and involves the visualization, intention, and result described above.

Third, white light emanates from the TAM in your heart, from which a white offering goddess manifests. As before, this white offering goddess emanates thousands of offering goddesses just like herself. They are very elegant and beautiful. All of them make offerings of loose flowers to Tara and her retinue, adorning the graceful and brilliant body of the *yeshe sempa* with flowers. The flowers are of various sizes, and have the most exquisite colors, shapes, and fragrances. The celestial palace is also filled with many beautiful flowers. Many of these flowers are forming by themselves, making the

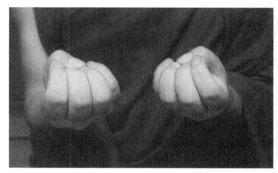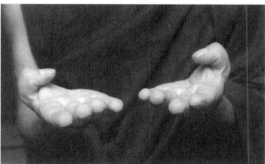

flower offering mudra ~ PUKPE

offering continuous and immeasurable. As before, the offering is not made because Tara has attachment to beautiful flowers. Instead, the merit of such an offering results on a relative level in beings obtaining a beautiful form or outer appearance. The ultimate benefit is that all beings will become adorned with the greater and lesser physical marks and signs of enlightenment, just as the Buddha did. You make the offering with the aspiration that all beings attain enlightenment and acquire such physical attributes. Again, as with the first two offerings, the mantra, the mudra, and the visualization must all go together. The mantra is OM BEDZRA PUKPE AH HUNG. The mudra in this case is the gesture of throwing flowers.

The next offering is of all precious things that have a soothing, uplifting fragrance. In Tibetan, the word *toksay* describes a mixture of all such ingredients. Like incense, it is a combination of the all the best mixed together. Again, from the TAM in your heart a dark blue light emanates, from which a dark blue goddess appears. As before, she emanates many goddesses like herself, and they offer incense to the *yeshe sempa* and

incense offering mudra ~ DHUPE

her retinue in the sky in front. Through the merit of making this offering, whatever bad smells there are in the worlds of beings are completely eliminated. This refers to the bad smells that sentient beings emit, the repulsive odors in the lower realms of existence, and so on. As a result, the surroundings of all beings are filled with the most soothing and clarifying air. Again, the mantra, visualization, and mudra must go together. The mantra is OM BEDZRA DHUPE AH HUNG. The mudra is like holding incense.

Fifth, from the syllable TAM in your heart, a light red light is emanated. A light red offering goddess appears, and emanates many thousands more like herself. All of these goddesses make offerings of lamps to the *yeshe sempa* and her retinue in front. These lamps are radiating a purifying light. This light is the embodiment of all light and all the sources of light that bring illumination into the world. Relatively, through the merit of this offering the suffering of any form of darkness that beings experience

light offering mudra ~ ALOKE

is eliminated, such as in realms where no light penetrates. For example, in the lower realms of existence, many beings are deprived of everything that gives light, and suffer from total darkness. It brings light so that they can see. It also brings light to those who experience darkness because of blindness. Ultimately, by the merit of this offering the darkness of ignorance of all beings without exception is eliminated. The true lamp of wisdom is ignited in the minds of all beings. That lamp of wisdom is the fruit of freedom from the darkness of ignorance. With the mantra OM BEDZRA ALOKE AH HUNG, the mudra is like the container of the lamp with the flame sticking out. The thumbs represent the tongues of flame.

Sixth, from the TAM in your heart, green light rays emanate, from which a green offering goddess appears. She emanates many graceful and beautiful offering goddesses just like herself. They all have perfumed water in their hands. This is the essence of whatever produces the best perfume. With both of their hands, each goddess offers perfumed water to the bodies of *yeshe sempa* and her retinue. With a sincere attitude, you should aspire that the fruit of the merit of this offering will be to remove the stains, here identified with odors, caused by immoral conduct, by breaking vows of moral conduct, and by conduct lacking moral discipline. Think that the stains as well as the harm they produce are removed. With the mantra OM BEDZRA GENDHE AH HUNG, the mudra is as if you have perfume on your fingertips and are applying it. Again, the

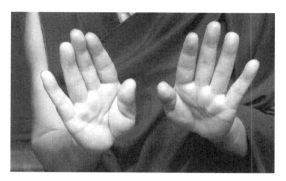

perfumed water offering mudra ~ GENDHE

three things go together: the mantra, the mudra, and the visualization.

Some clarification is needed here. The offering of incense is for relative benefit. Through the merit of offering incense, unpleasant odors such as those emitted by sentient beings and those present in the lower states of existence are removed. The offering of perfumed water, on the other hand, is of ultimate benefit. Through the merit of this offering, beings become free from the stains of having broken moral discipline. In this case there is only ultimate benefit.

Seventh, from the syllable TAM in your heart yellow light radiates, and from this a yellow offering goddess appears and she, too, manifests thousands of beautiful goddesses like herself. They all make offerings of food to the *yeshe sempa* and her retinue in beautiful vessels made from precious stones of all kinds. This is the essence of the

most precious of foods in the realms of gods and humans from the standpoint of cleanliness, nutritive value, and healing. The result of this offering is that all beings obtain freedom from hunger and deprivation, particularly the beings in the lower realms. Therefore on a relative level it frees all beings of immediate hunger and eliminates its causes. Ultimately, we aspire that all sentient beings without exception never again

food offering mudra ~ NEWIDYE

have to depend on relative sources of existence. This is the wish that they realize and experience perfect enlightenment and therefore become able to live on the inexhaustible food of samadhi, the food of meditative realization. The mantra is OM BEDZRA NEWIDYE AH HUNG, and the mudra is a gesture of holding the food respectfully.

Finally, from the syllable TAM in your heart light blue, almost grayish-blue, light radiates and from that a grayish-blue offering goddess appears. She is graceful and beautiful, and emanates many offering goddesses just like herself. All of them make the offering of sound. This is the best of all music and whatever musical instruments that produce them, as well as every beautiful sound and the objects that produce them. Through the virtue and goodness of this offering, all sounds that bring harm are eliminated. Words that bring fear, such as "kill," "hurt," or "cut" are unheard. In the hell realms the suffering is so extreme that whatever suffering we experience does not compare. Even just the sounds that are heard there cause intense suffering. This, and all sounds everywhere that cause suffering or fear of any kind – whether produced by nature or by people intentionally or unintentionally – are purified and completely removed.

In its place, the world, the universe, the minds, and the surroundings of all beings are filled with wholesome sounds. All sounds are beautiful to hear and soothing. They are the sounds of truth, the sounds of goodness, the sounds that foster well-being and harmony. They fill all space. Ultimately, all sound is the sound of Dharma. This is not limited only to the vehicle of speech and the voice of a spiritual friend who teaches Dharma. Whatever sounds occur are nothing other than the sounds of Dharma. The Dharma is self-uttering, whether it be through the singing of birds, the rattling of leaves, the wind, or anything else. Those of you familiar with the Amitabha practice know that it takes place in a pure buddhafield. Just as in Amitabha's pure land, whatever

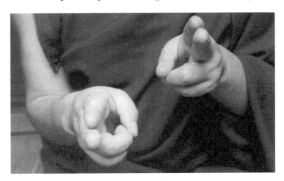

music offering mudra ~ SHABDA

sounds that occur are only the sounds of Dharma. The essential point is to turn your mind to hear the sound of the Dharma. For this offering, the mantra is OM BEDZRA SHABDA AH HUNG. The corresponding mudra is like the beating of a round drum. This represents all instruments that make sound. The reason for using this particular mudra is that Buddhist ritual sadhana practices are preceded by a drum. The drum starts it and the other instruments follow.

At the end of this period of presenting offerings, think that all of the offering goddesses dissolve back into your own heart. Then, through the auspiciousness and virtue of having made these eight offerings to the *yeshe sempa*, the wisdom deity dissolves into light and merges with you. In this way, the wisdom deity and the self-visualized deity become inseparable. That inseparability is expressed by the mantra DZA HUNG BAM HO. This is accompanied by a mudra, which is a gesture indicating that front and back, top and bottom, you have become inseparable.

four mudras corresponding (in sequence) to DZA HUNG BAM HO

What follows in Tibetan is NYI SU MAY PAR GYUR and a mudra meaning that the *yeshe sempa* and *damtsig sempa* are not two. They have become one. It is like water dissolving into water. The water is one substance, and cannot be separated. Although it cannot be separated, its volume has become greater. You become more radiant than ever. It is like turning up a lamp so that it gives more light. Think that until enlightenment, the wisdom deity will never leave you.

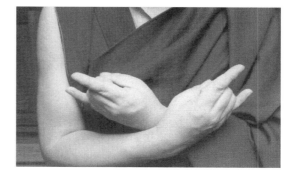

mudra accompanying NYI SU MAY PAR GYUR

Having dissolved the wisdom deity into yourself as Tara, you think, "I have now actually become Tara. I possess all of Tara's qualities." Even though in your physical perception your flesh-and-blood body has not literally disappeared, you stop attending to it, and you identify with this image of the visualized Tara. You regard yourself as possessing all of the attributes and characteristics of the deity. You look like her, and have her mind, ornamentation, attire, and so on. You actually are Tara.

Empowerment and Complete Accomplishment

The next part of the practice is empowering yourself as the deity. This begins with light radiating from the TAM syllable in the center of your heart once again. This time the light goes in specific directions. One portion of the light rays goes to the front of you, which is regarded as east. It does not matter if you are actually physically facing east or not – you regard the front to be east. Another portion goes to your right, another behind you, another to your left, and another goes above you. Through this you invite the buddhas of the five families together with their retinues from these four quadrants and the upper region of the universe. As the light rays reach these buddhas of the five families in their places of residence, you think that the light rays themselves become offering substances, which please and respectfully invite these buddhas to come and bestow empowerment.

Accepting your invitation, the five buddhas appear above you in the space in front, each accompanied by a great retinue. Principal among the retinue are the male and female bodhisattvas, dakas and dakinis, and male and female wrathful deities. The buddhas are the father Buddha Vairocana (*Nampar Nangdze*) and the mother Buddha Dhatvishvari (*Yangkyi Wangchungma*); the father Buddha Akshobhya (*Mikyöpa*) and the mother Buddha Mamaki; the father Buddha Ratnasambhava (*Rinchen Jungden*) and the mother Buddha Buddhalochana (*Sangyechenma*); the father Buddha Amitabha (*Nangwa Thaye*) and the mother Buddha Pandaravasini (*Gökarma*); and the father Buddha Amoghasiddhi (*Dönyö Drubpa*) and the mother Buddha Samayatara (*Damtsig Drolma*).[24] They are what is called *yab yum. Yab* is honorific for "father." *Yum* is honorific for "mother." The buddhas are arranged in the following way: In the center is Vairocana; in front, in the east, is Akshobya; to the south is Ratnasambhava; behind, in the west, is Amitabha; and in the north is Amoghasiddhi.

Then, in the same way as you made offerings of drinking water, bathing water, flowers, incense, light, perfumed water, food, and music to the *yeshe sempa* previously, you now make offerings to the five buddhas and their retinues. The mantra for that is OM PENTSAKULA (referring to the five) SAPARIWARA (referring to the assemblage) and then each offering. For each of the eight kinds of offerings, there are as many offering goddesses as there are deities and retinue, and each deity receives individual offerings.

Then you request empowerment from the lords of the five buddha families with the mantra SARWA TATHAGATA ABIKENTSA TU MUM, which means "May all the Tathagatas grant me empowerment." Having made this supplication, you should have a sense that your request is being acknowledged and that the buddhas will empower you. Then you think that the deities bestow empowerment in the following way:

First, in response to your request the five buddhas enter into a state of meditation, and in this state they bestow upon you the actual or ultimate empowerment. The actual words of empowerment that you say when reciting the liturgy and that you imagine are being said by the five male buddhas as they empower you are, "Just as at the time of the [Buddha's] birth he received ablution from the devas, in the same way I bestow [upon you] a bath of pure celestial waters."

This refers to a miraculous event that took place immediately after the Buddha was born. When he came forth from his mother's side, his majesty and radiance were so great that no human being dared to touch him. Gods and goddesses appeared spontaneously and offered cleansing baths of celestial waters to the Buddha, dried his body with celestial silks, and offered him praises. Whenever empowerment is performed, this event is referred to. What the empowerment deities are saying is that just as the Buddha at birth was washed in that way, so I wash you with this, the water of empowerment.

The five female buddhas take up precious vases filled with wisdom ambrosia and they physically empower you by pouring the ambrosia into you through the aperture at the top of your head. While the mother buddhas do this, the male and female bodhisattvas express the auspiciousness of the empowerment by casting rains of flowers upon you, dancing, and singing praises. The male and female wrathful deities guard the perimeter, ensuring that no obstacles arise to interfere with the process of empowerment.

As the five mother buddhas are pouring the ambrosia from the five vases into the top of your head, you should visualize that your body is filling up with pure nectar. Eventually it fills your entire body, purifying all obscurations. The mother buddhas continue to pour, and the excess overflows at the crown of your head and is transformed into Buddha Amitabha, who becomes your crown ornament. Though the empowerment is bestowed by all five buddha families, you are crowned with Amitabha, who is the lord of the family to which Tara belongs. Generally speaking, though, he embodies all five families.

The empowerment having been completed, the male and female wrathful ones dissolve into the male and female bodhisattvas. They, in turn dissolve into light and melt into the mother buddhas. Then the five mother buddhas dissolve into light and merge into the five male buddhas. Then among these five buddhas, four of them dissolve into Buddha Amitabha, who dissolves into the Buddha Amitabha above your head.

What is of principal importance throughout the process of empowerment is to let go of the identification of yourself with your ordinary perception of the physical body as a coarse and imperfect flesh and blood body, and identification of your mind with what you ordinarily experience it to be. In the development stage you are attempting to relinquish these fixations and replace them with identification with the deity.

As you advance in this practice, you will be able to appreciate its profundity more and more. You will be able to see and experience its skillful means. For instance, having started as the *damtsig sempa*, and invoking and becoming inseparable from the *yeshe sempa*, you finally merge with the assembly of buddhas and bodhisattvas. You become the embodiment of them all.

At this point it is appropriate to think, "I really am Tara." This is a state beyond everything in samsara and nirvana. There is nothing beyond it. Consequently, there is nothing outside yourself to which you can make offerings. Therefore, to acknowledge the fact that you really are the deity, you make offerings to the Tara you have become, the Tara who is the essence of all buddhas. This is the final part of the development stage of the practice.

As before, you emanate from the seed syllable in your heart offering goddesses who hold the same eight offering substances that were offered previously to the *yeshe sempa*, and you imagine that they present these to you as Tara. The offering mantra they say is OM ARYA TARA SAPARIWARA. As you know from the previous offering mantra, SAPARIWARA refers to the assemblage. The five mother and five father buddhas and their retinues have become inseparable from you and you are now crowned with Amitabha, who embodies them all. So, in form you are Tara, but in essence you are all of them. The offering mantra expresses this.

Then all eight main offering goddesses gather together and as one offer praises to you in beautiful melodious voices as you yourself chant the praises in the liturgy. As you see in the text, they sing, "with crowns on their heads, gods and asuras (demigods) bow at the lotus feet" of Tara. Gods and asuras are mentioned because ordinarily beings look up to gods as the ultimate – as saviors and protectors. As a symbol of their high birth and power they even have jeweled crowns. Therefore, even the beings that are considered to be supreme in this universe offer their respect to Tara with the highest part of their body, their crowns. With that highest part they touch the feet, the lowest part, of Tara, acknowledging her enlightened qualities. If the gods look up to Tara in this way, there is no need to say how the rest of beings should look up to her. Thus all sentient beings are implied. This expression means that Tara is incomparable. No sentient being in any realm can compare with her.

The reason that she is offered this highest respect is expressed by the next line of the praise, which says, "We prostrate and make praises to the liberating mother, who delivers beings from all misfortune." The term *pongpa* here is often understood to mean "impoverishment" or "loss," but it means more than that. It refers to the experience of deprivation or misfortune, which in the broadest sense can include basically everything we regard as suffering, whether material or spiritual. For those who go to them for protection, the gods may be able to bring some benefit, but it is only temporary benefit. Since the gods themselves are not free, they cannot help anyone attain complete liberation. In contrast, Tara can liberate us from any and all misfortune or deprivation, and bring us to a state of perfect enlightenment. Therefore all pay homage to and praise Tara, the mother of all buddhas.

Having completed the offerings and praises, the offering goddesses dissolve back into your heart. In that way, your unification with the deity is complete, as has been acknowledged by the offering goddesses. This concludes the development stage (*kyerim*) of the practice.

The Three Characteristics of Good Kyerim *Practice*

Perseverance is essential during *kyerim* practice. *Kyerim* must also have three important characteristics. The first is *sal* or *sel* (it can be pronounced either way), which means "clarity." The second is *dak*, which means "purity." The third is *ten*, or "stability." We should make the commitment to fulfill these three characteristics, because only by fulfilling these elements can we do justice to the practice.

The first, *sal*, means bringing as much clarity, vividness, and brilliance as you can to the visualization. Your visualization should be like the reflection in a clean mirror – complete, clear, and vivid, just as it is; or like a good painting so that the painted object looks like the real object.

The second is *dak*, or purity as it pertains to pure view. This means that while doing the visualization you recognize that the visualized deity is not a substantial entity. It is merely the appearance of the deity, like a rainbow, and has no substantial existence as such anywhere. If you fall into conceptual fixation about a form, sound, taste, or feeling, this can distort the visualization. It leads to concepts such as, "This form is bad," "That form is good," and so on. If such concepts arise, you should view them as empty and insubstantial – in essence nothing other than the wisdom display of the deity.

The third one is stability, or *ten*, which means the stable confidence or stable pride of recognizing that you actually are the deity. Stability means not merely thinking, "I am visualizing myself as Tara," or "I am imagining myself to be Tara," but instead thinking, "I actually am Tara. I really possess all of the attributes and characteristics of Tara." Ordinary defiled concepts such as "I don't deserve to be Tara," or "I have so many shortcomings. How can I be Tara?", or "I am just a beginner," and so forth are absent. It is crucial to abandon these kinds of ordinary concepts.

These are the three characteristics of good *kyerim* practice. All three are equally important, but special attention must be paid to the purity and stability aspects, which are absolutely essential in working with the practice.

~

Student: Initially, when we dissolve everything into emptiness, should we think of everything as a black void?

Rinpoche: A black void would not be emptiness. It would be something, because black is something. It is a characteristic. Emptiness is the nature of all things irrespective of characteristics. Therefore, instead of trying to imagine emptiness, what you do is simply relinquish concepts about the characteristics of phenomena, and you imagine that the protection circle, palace, lotus, moon, and all other aspects of the visualization emerge from or are the expression of that nature that is beyond fixation on characteristics.

I will give you a rough analogy for this. With your eye, look at your eye and tell me what it is like. You have to make your eye look right at your eye. There is nothing you can say in response to that. It is beyond expression and beyond any kind of response. Then look at things with your eyes, and of course you can see things. Things appear. That is like the appearance of things within the nature of emptiness. This is just an analogy. It is not the same as emptiness.

Student: When we visualize ourselves as Tara, do we also visualize Tara outside ourselves as well?

Rinpoche: With the understanding that the TAM is the essence of your own mind, to say that the TAM becomes Tara is to say that you become Tara. Unlike some other practices where there is both frontal and self-visualization, here there is only yourself visualized as Tara.

The Main Practice:
Mantra Recitation (Ngagrim)

*N*ow we turn to the second part of the practice, which is the recitation of the mantra. Through recitation of the mantra, you gradually cause yourself to receive the blessings and power of the mantra. For this second phase of the practice there are some additional visualizations, the first of which is a more elaborate visualization in your heart.

Trying your best to fulfill the three characteristics of clarity, purity, and stability, visualize in the center of your heart a many-petaled lotus as you did before. On this is a moon disk and on that there is a white wheel with eight spokes. This white eight-spoked wheel looks very much like a ship's wheel, except that it ends with the rim. It does not have the knobs sticking out of it the way the rim of a ship's wheel does. The wheel is lying flat on top of the moon. It is luminous and empty like a rainbow.

On the center of the hub of the wheel stands a white syllable TAM, just barely touching. Above the TAM is the syllable OM, and below the TAM and the hub is the syllable HA. There is space between the hub of the wheel and the moon disk, so the HA is not touching either one of them.

The long-life mantra is arranged around the syllable TAM on the edge of the hub in a clockwise direction (facing inward), standing like pins on a pin cushion: OM MAMA AYU PUNYE JNANA PUKTRIM KURU HA. For most mother tantra deities the mantra garland is clockwise and if it spins, it spins in the opposite direction, or counterclockwise. Likewise, most of the deities of the father tantra have counterclockwise mantra garlands which face outward and turn in a clockwise direction if there is motion.

OM

TAM

HA

The syllable MAMA means "me," and remains in the mantra garland when you are doing it as a daily practice or for your own longevity. If you are doing it to lengthen the life of your guru, however, then instead of visualizing and saying MAMA, you can replace it with the word GURU. Similarly, when you are doing it for someone else's longevity, then you can replace it with that person's name. If you are uncomfortable with changing the mantra, however, it is also all right to leave it just as it is. It will be just as effective either way. What the mantra means is as follows: AYU means "life." PUNYE means "merit." JNANA means "wisdom." PUKTRIM KURU means "increase." Its meaning is very straightforward.

OM   MAMA   AYU   PUNYE   JNANA   PUKTRIM   KURU   HA

Though the mantra wheel has OM MAMA AYU PUNYE JNANA PUKTRIM KURU HA, you recite OM TARE TUTTARE TURE MAMA AYU PUNYE JNANA PUKTRIM KURU SOHA during the special long-life recitation of the practice. It is necessary to say the SO when reciting this mantra, but according to the mandala of the Tara practice the SO does not appear in the long-life mantra circle in the heart.

Each spoke of the wheel appears somewhat like a dorje, starting to taper at the hub, getting bigger in the middle, and then tapering down again to the rim. On the top of the belly of each spoke at its widest point is a syllable of the root mantra, TA RE TUT TA RE TU RE SO, each standing like a pin on a pin cushion and facing inward.

TA   RE   TUT   TA   RE   TU   RE   SO

All of these syllables, the TAM in the center and the two circles of mantra, remain motionless. They are all brilliantly white, shining like pearls, and they radiate a great deal of light.

Recitation of the Root Mantra

There are two aspects to the mantra repetition. There is what you are doing verbally and there is what you are doing with your mind. The things to avoid in the verbal repetition are incorrect pronounciation and slurring. Also, it should not be repeated too quickly nor too slowly. You should be able to hear the sound as you recite it, but avoid repeating it too loudly so that you are bellowing it, or too quietly so that you are not saying it at all.

What you do with your mind is as follows: Recitation of the mantra activates the syllables on the mantra wheel. Through the activity of your speech as you recite the short root mantra of Tara, OM TARE TUTTARE TURE SOHA, all the syllables on the mantra wheel become more and more radiant, glowing brighter and brighter. Then light radiates out, principally from the TAM but also from the mantras surrounding it, and makes immeasurable offerings to all the buddhas and bodhisattvas in the ten directions and three times. Having made offerings, the light returns with their blessings, and the syllables become even brighter than before.

Again light radiates out, benefiting all the beings in every realm in myriad ways. Principally, their life force and their life spans are augmented, but the benefit is not limited to that. Each being receives an abundance of whatever they need, and each is enriched with knowledge and wisdom. The benefit is immeasurable and inconceivable.

When the light returns, as the fruit of the excellent merit accumulated from having made these offerings and benefited beings, it brings with it the blessings of all the buddhas and bodhisattvas, the relative and ultimate siddhis of beings, and the pure vital essence of the world and of beings of both samsara and nirvana. You receive both the relative and the ultimate quintessence of life and vitality of the entire universe and the beings contained in it, collected in the form of light.

The scope of this is vast, including all that is a part of cyclic existence and held by all beings, all that exists in the inanimate world, and also all that is beyond cyclic existence such as the quintessence of the vitality of the buddhas, bodhisattvas, arhats, and so forth. All of this dissolves into the seed syllable TAM in your heart. As it does so, the seed syllable and mantra circles, which were very bright before, become even brighter, even more lustrous, even more radiant. You accomplish the siddhi of deathlessness.

It is important to understand that you are not stealing anything here. You are not taking away the quintessence of the vitality of others and leaving them short. In fact, what is happening is that the emanated light rays augment the vitality of other beings so much that they now have more than they need. The entire world has become filled with vitality, bursting with vitality, and there is so much of it that some of it comes back with the light rays to you. Therefore, far from stealing, you have actually augmented the vitality and life of others. Meditating on that, you repeat the mantra.

While repeating the mantra continuously, your mind works on the larger visualization, which in time will become clearer and clearer. For beginners it is difficult at first to do a clear visualization while chanting the liturgy, so during the mantra it is important to work on the *kyerim* visualization. You can begin with the visualization of the vajra protection tent from the seed syllable and then the progressive visualizations leading to the appearance of the deity, dwelling on each detail until it becomes very clear.

Later, when your mind is more stable, you will be able to do the *kyerim* visualizations as you chant them in the liturgy. Then you will be able to spend time during the mantra refining the self-visualization and palace by going over it again and again to make it more clear and vivid, developing the firm pride that you are the deity.

It is not the intention of a practice like this to rest your mind upon any one aspect of the practice for too long, because that is too difficult. Therefore, even though the liturgy describes the emanation and gathering of light rays during the mantra, in practice this is only one aspect of your visualization. The best approach is to move from one aspect of the visualization to another. For example, initially during the mantra you should review the basic visualization of yourself as Tara, of her environment, and so forth, so that you have a strong sense of the context. Then rest your mind as one-pointedly as possible on the visualization of the wheel, seed syllable, and mantras in the heart. At some point you will find that this becomes stale and your mind becomes restless. Then you should apply the emanation and gathering of light rays as described in the liturgy.

When your mind becomes weary of that, you can simply rest it one-pointedly on the sound of the mantra as you continue to repeat it, or you can direct your attention back to various aspects of the visualization of the deity's form in turn. In this way your self-visualization becomes clearer and clearer as you focus on a particular ornament, a particular feature, and so on, generating clarity with regard to that part of the visualization and then moving on to another detail. From time to time return again to the radiation and gathering of light rays. In that way do not try to force your mind to stay put for too long on any one aspect, but move gently from one aspect of the practice to another.

Vajrayana teachings seem very complex and difficult to understand on the one hand, but on the other hand, because of skillful means they are simple and very profound. Also, if you know one sadhana practice very well, it helps you to understand others because there are similarities in the meanings of the various elements. As the great master Karma Chagme Rinpoche has said, it is like cutting a bamboo tree. When you cut one, you know the particular joint where to cut and you know that the inside is hollow. After that you will understand the characteristics of bamboo trees and know that all other bamboo trees are also hollow.

The Commitments and Benefits of the Practice

To complete the mantra recitation, we do one million recitations of the root mantra. Normally 100,000 repetitions are done for each syllable of a mantra. The root mantra of Tara has ten syllables, so this is how the number one million is determined. One million is the minimum prerequisite that enables us to begin to use the practice to benefit others. When we talk about the completion of the mantra recitation (this one million or the later ten million), we are talking about doing it in one stretch of time, such as in retreat. This is referred to in Tibetan parlance as "on one seat." This does not mean 10,000 here, 20,000 there, over the years, but in a retreat situation or in one stretch of time.

When a genuine practitioner has properly done ten million repetitions, they should be able to accomplish all four activities to benefit beings (pacifying, enriching, magnetizing, and subduing). They are then a *dorje lobpön,* or vajra master. The vajra master is someone who can manifest the four activities properly and through this bring great benefit to others. A genuine practitioner is someone who pays sincere attention to the practice and has pure devotion. These are the qualities every good practitioner should have. If, on the contrary, one recites the mantra but is distracted or lacks devotion, there will be no such accomplishment.

As I said, in order for someone to become a *dorje lobpön,* the minimum accomplishment is ten million mantra recitations for each tantric deity whose empowerment they give. Another requirement is in terms of time. Depending on the situation and the teacher one is involved with, one makes a commitment of time. A minimum of five years is required, but it could be anywhere between five to ten years that one commits oneself to do the practice of that particular yidam. Of course, a practitioner with that kind of commitment can do many more than ten million recitations of the mantra. This is just the minimum requirement to be able to assume the role of vajra master.

The highest or true vajra master is one for whom there is no discussion of numbers or time. Instead, he or she does that particular practice until experiencing a vision of the deity. In Tibetan this is known as *shel dalwa* – seeing the deity face-to-face. This is the complete realization of the deity. All the lineage holders for this practice are true *dorje lobpöns,* who accomplished the practice, realized the deity, and truly accomplish the benefit of others.

In our own case, it is good if we relate to the practice in all three ways – in terms of numbers, time, and signs of realization. First, we should make the commitment to say the mantra ten million times, since ten million recitations of the root mantra is the accomplishment of the mantra and not only fulfills the mantra but accomplishes the activities of the mantra. This is the lowest commitment, so we do not have to stop there.

Second, we can commit to doing the practice for a certain period of time. During this time we will probably recite the mantra even more than the fixed number of times. Third, we can make the commitment to continue until we have achieved the marks of realization. This would be a commitment to continue until we encounter Tara face-to-face. This commitment can last our whole life. Since the commitment is to practice until the signs and marks of realization occur, if we die before we have seen Tara, we would not give up at death.

This practice can also be done in order to accomplish more immediate relative benefits. It can be done to clear away obstacles or improve our own situation; for example, it can clear away the obstacle of sickness. For that, a retreat for a minimum of seven days with completely sincere devotion and diligence can overcome whatever obstacles there might be. This is said in the commentary on the practice, and I can vouch for it based on my own personal experience as well as on having seen its success for other practitioners.

I have no wish to make spurious claims of realization, but I must tell you the truth about the effectiveness of this practice. For some reason – I am not really sure why – from the earliest days I can remember, I was always convinced that I would die at the age of sixty. I used to hear these words in my head, "I will die at sixty," almost as though I were saying it to myself. I never received this as a prophecy. No one predicted it, and I didn't have a vision or anything. It is just that from the time I was a small child, I was certain of this. Later, after I grew up, I met several lamas from whom I received teachings. A number of them told me they felt I would not live longer than sixty years.

Sure enough, when I approached the age of sixty I started to have serious health problems. One thing after another added up to a pretty scary situation. I approached the great teacher Kalu Rinpoche and asked him what I should do about it. Both he and later H.E. Gyaltsap Rinpoche strongly recommended that I do a month-long White Tara retreat. Neither of them said that if I did this, I would overcome the obstacles and live longer. They just told me to do it. I felt that I should follow their advice, so I went into retreat in the building I was living at the time and started to do the practice.

During the first fifteen days it became increasingly difficult, and finally nearly impossible. I grew more and more terrified. I wondered what could be in the house with me. I did not see or hear anything that could possibly justify or cause such a state of anxiety. Nevertheless, I found myself in a state of complete panic. I became very concerned and was at a loss to know what to do. I changed my bed around a few times, but that was no help. Regardless, I kept doing the practice. During the last half of the month, however, things began cooling off. The panic, fear, and terror started to dissipate. Things slowly returned to normal, and I was able to complete the practice.

What I went through was quite serious. It has been many years since I completed that practice. I am now seventy-eight years old and still continue to be in good health. I regard the fact that I am still here as the blessing of the lineage and the result of having done this practice. Therefore I have deep confidence in this practice from the perspective of personal experience.

I do not think that there is anything magical about the lineage or the deity or the teaching. I think that the key is entrusting yourself to them utterly. What causes the differences in how much benefit you achieve by doing a practice is the degree to which you actually open yourself to the practice and entrust yourself to it completely. As long as you do not do that, you are like a vessel that is covered. If the top is not taken off, then no matter how much you pour over it, nothing will go into it. If you are able to apply these practices with confidence and sincerity, however, the effectiveness of the practice is unquestionable.

The Commentary: The Three Types of Recitation

We will now turn to Jamgön Kongrul's commentary on the practice. It describes three ways of working with the mantra, which are known as the three kinds of recitation. In all of them the visualizations of yourself as the deity, the mantra wheel, and the syllables remain the same as discussed previously.

The first type of recitation is known in Tibetan as *gong depa*. Here you do not recite the mantra verbally. The focus of the mind in this case is on the self-sound of the mantra. The mantra reverberates with its own sound. It is like, for instance, when metal is struck. You are not making the sound; the activity is making the sound. It is like a wind chime, which is self-sounding. Like that, focus your mind on the mantra circles, on the mantra syllables emanating light, and on the self-sound of the mantra.

The second type of recitation is called *dorje depa*. Additional special instructions are necessary in order to do this, but I am including it here so that you will have it when you need it. Here again there is no verbal recitation involved. Instead, when breathing out, the light radiating from the TAM goes out and makes offerings to the buddhas and bodhisattvas in all directions and benefits all beings in all realms everywhere. When breathing in, the rays return to the TAM in the heart, bringing with them the enlightened qualities and blessings of the buddhas and bodhisattvas and the vital essence of the universe and of beings. During the periods between inhalation and exhalation, one holds the breath briefly, and during this time, the focus is on the TAM in the heart.

The *dorje depa* involves a particular method in which the breath is held in the region of the navel. This is a different kind of relationship with the breath – not the way we normally breathe. When done properly, it is an excellent practice. Again, special instructions are necessary in order to do this, and it should not be attempted without them. Though it involves working in relation to the breath, this does not mean that one is working *on* the breath. One uses the breath while focusing on the syllable TAM and the light going out from and returning to the TAM. In the future when it is appropriate you will receive this instruction.

Finally, the commentary describes a third kind of repetition, known as *tro du depa*, and this is the way we will do the practice. Your body, speech, and mind are all involved with the repetition of the mantra. Your speech makes the sound, your hands use the mala, and your mind focuses on the visualizations of the rays going out, returning, and so forth. It is important to maintain mindfulness of every aspect of the meditation.

This visualization is twofold, which is not as clear in the practice text that I explained earlier as it is in the commentary on the practice. The commentary explains that there are two parts to this visualization, each part with two phases.

First, as you recite the mantra, light rays emanate out in all directions from the TAM and mantra circles, and make immeasurable offerings to the buddhas and bodhisattvas. The offerings are whatever is worthy of being offered – whatever pleases the body, speech, and mind of all the buddhas and bodhisattvas. In some practices this visualization is very elaborate, involving offering goddesses coming from each light ray and offering different things. However, here it is much simpler. The light is the embodiment of all worthy offerings. It is not necessary to conceptualize about what may be a worthy offering or how large the offerings are. Then, having made these offerings, the light returns to the TAM in your heart along with the blessings and wisdom of all the buddhas and bodhisattvas.

In the second phase of the first part of the visualization, the light radiates out again and benefits all beings everywhere. Though Tara is often practiced with the intention of increasing longevity, her activity is not limited to just that. The light performs every conceivable benefit – whatever is needed or helpful to sentient beings, including leading them to supreme enlightenment. When the light returns to the TAM and mantra circle, it brings with it the merit accumulated through these offerings and benefit.

The second part of the visualization has two phases as well. First, light emanates out and goes to all inanimate objects in the outer world – to the rocks, lakes, trees, etc. When the light strikes them, their vitality is greatly enhanced. Then the light returns to the TAM and mantra circle, bringing with it the vital essence of everything inanimate. It is like lighting a lamp from another lamp. The second lamp is lit, but the first lamp has not been diminished in any way nor has it gone out.

In phase two, the light radiates out again, this time going to all beings – the animate – which is referred to in the Tibetan by the expression *yo* ("whatever moves"). This light greatly enhances the wholesome vitality of all beings. Then the wholesome essence of all beings (wisdom, knowledge, health, and all wholesome qualities) returns with the rays and melts into the TAM and mantra garland, which blaze even brighter with vitality. These essences are coming to you without taking anything away from beings. Again, it is like one lamp lighting another.

In this way, you work first with the essence of the inanimate world and then with the essence of sentient beings in the two phases of this second part. What exactly is it that is being collected from the inanimate and animate? All animate and inanimate objects are composed of the elements: earth, water, fire, air, and space. When there is a balance between the elements in the living physical body, the factors that sustain the body remain intact and the body remains strong and healthy. When there is an imbalance or diminishing of these elements, then strength is lost and one becomes susceptible to illness and other problems.

It is the same in nature. When trees and plants have rich sources of the elements and those elements are in proper balance, there is nurturing and growth. Without this, growth diminishes or stops and things deteriorate. All inanimate objects, even precious stones and metals, contain the essence of the elements as well. Thus the vital essence of beings and the world refers to the elements, and here we are concerned with the essence of those elements. That is what is being collected.

Among the three types of recitation, the first two (the *gong depa* and the *dorje depa*) are for advanced practitioners who have a great deal of control over their minds and control over their mind-body continuum. Therefore, right now we are only doing the third, the *tro du depa*.

Recitation of the Long-Life Mantra

During regular practice, you normally recite the long-life mantra OM TARE TUTTARE TURE MAMA AHYU PUNYE JNANA PUKTRIM KURU SO HA one-tenth as many times as the root mantra. Therefore if you recite the ten-syllable root mantra one thousand times, you would recite the long-life mantra one hundred times. There is a special visualization for the long-life practice as well.

With regard to applying this practice to your own longevity, the self-visualization is the same as previously described. You visualize yourself as Tara, and just as before, you are crowned with Amitabha, who is the essence of the five buddha families. Then, with a sincere and mindful attitude you earnestly request Amitabha on the crown of your head to grant you the siddhi of long life. He is pleased to acknowledge your sincere request, and from the HRI in his heart he emanates light, which goes to all the buddhas and bodhisattvas in the ten directions and three times.

The light returns with their blessings, relative and ultimate siddhis, and the relative and ultimate quintessence of samsara and nirvana. When it returns, it enters the begging bowl Amitabha is holding in his two hands in the form of white amrita. This amrita begins to boil in the begging bowl and then overflows and enters you through the crown of your head. It is not painful when it enters you. It is not like boiling oil. It boils and bubbles and flows over the rim of the begging bowl. It fills your whole body completely. For as long as you continue to recite the long mantra, you continue with the visualization of it boiling over and overflowing and filling your body completely. Your appearance becomes ever more radiant and glowing.

If you want to accomplish someone else's longevity there would be no change in the words of the liturgy, but there would be a change in the visualization. In this case there is a simple way and a more elaborate way to do it. The elaborate way should be used for your teachers or other persons for whom you have devotion or great respect. It starts at the beginning of the practice when we form the initial self-visualization of Tara. You do the entire *kyerim* visualization for both yourself and the other person simultaneously. Finally, both of you appear in the form of Tara, complete with ornamentation and so on. It does not matter where you place the other person - in front, to the right, or to the left. Do whatever is most comfortable. However, be careful not to mistake this for a self and frontal

Amitabha

visualization. You develop two parallel visualizations because its purpose is to benefit the other person.

When you get to the long-life section, Amitabha is on your head as Tara and Amitabha is also on the other person's head as Tara. When you make the request to Amitabha, the request is acknowledged by both the Amitabha on your crown and the Amitabha on the other person's crown. The amrita overflows from both begging bowls and fills both your body and his or her body simultaneously.

The other way is simpler. You do the practice exactly the same way as you did for your own longevity. Amitabha's begging bowl is filled, overflows, and fills you as Tara. Visualize the person you are helping in front of you in their ordinary form, facing you and slightly below you. Pray earnestly to Amitabha to grant the siddhi of long life to this person through you.

As Tara, you are the embodiment of the wisdom and awakened intelligence of all the buddhas and bodhisattvas. The amrita flows through your body completely and then flows out from the tips of the fingers of your right hand, which remains in the mudra of supreme generosity. The amrita enters the person through the crown of his or her head, filling their body and washing away all obstacles to long life and good health. Through this process of filling, all their obstacles and sickness drain out, and the person is completely cleansed. Finally, their entire body is completely filled with the glowing nectar of long life.

The normal daily practice described above, with the long-life mantra being recited one-tenth as many times as the root mantra, can accomplish longevity. However, when you are doing the Tara practice just for longevity – for example, if you or someone else is gravely ill – then the longer mantra should be the main mantra recitation.

This completes the second stage of the practice, the *ngagrim*.

~

Student: Does the light glow especially brilliantly just from the TAM, or just from the main six syllables, or just from the longer long-life mantra, or from all of them during these visualizations?

Rinpoche: Brilliant glowing light radiates from the TAM all the time. Otherwise, whatever mantra you are reciting is particularly glowing and radiant. When you are doing the visualizations of radiating light and collecting blessings and vital essences, the root mantra glows the most brightly. However, when you recite the long-life mantra, both mantras glow brilliantly because you are reciting both of them.

Student: When reciting the mantra, should you focus your attention mainly on the wheel and on each individual syllable as you recite it?

Rinpoche: Once in a while when you wish to clarify your visualization of the syllables, you can do this. But that is not the way you always work with it. When working with the mantra syllables, the main focus is on glowing and radiating light and, through this, making offerings, benefiting beings, and bringing back blessings and vital essences. But when you are working on developing the details of your visualization, then that is only one of the many details you can focus on.

Student: Do you have to do a complete visualization, including sending out the light, making offerings, and benefiting beings, and then collecting blessings and the vital essence of the world and beings with every recitation of the mantra in the *tro du depa*?

Rinpoche: What is important is all-around mindfulness. The number of mantras said by your mouth should correspond to the number of beads counted, and you should say the mantra completely and continuously while working on the visualization. The complete visualization does not have to correspond to each recitation of the mantra, but it must be done properly. That the visualization is proper and clear is what is important – not that the number of visualizations and mantras match.

Student: What kind of mala should be used to do this practice?

Rinpoche: For Tara practice it is best to use a bodhiseed mala. In fact, a bodhiseed mala is best for any practice. The second best for Tara practice is a karma mala or activity mala made of white conch, white crystal, or white coral. This kind of mala in other colors is also fine, such as blue. You should avoid using a mala made of animal horn or bone. There is one exception to this, but even then it is important to be careful. Sometimes in a practice for a wrathful deity under certain circumstances it might be good to use a bone mala. But in that situation it would have to be a bone mala made from the skull of a human being. The reason I am mentioning this is that Dharma materials are sold commercially now and you might be told that these malas are special or have mystic powers. However, you should avoid them.

Student: I am most interested in doing the practice for the long life of my lama. You mentioned earlier that when doing the long-life practice for your guru, you would substitute the word GURU for the word MAMA. Is that the most effective way to do it?

Rinpoche: The substitution of the word GURU in the mantra is optional. Even when you are doing the practice for someone else, you can say the mantra as it was originally written, without any substitution. Some people like to take out the word MAMA and put in the word GURU to remind themselves that they are doing it for the lama, but it does not matter, and it makes no difference insofar as the effectiveness of the practice is concerned.

The Main Practice:
The Completion Stage (Dzogrim)

*W*e have now completed two of the three parts of the main practice, the generation stage and the recitation of the mantra. The third part of the practice is called the completion stage (*dzogrim*), which in this case refers to the gradual withdrawal of the visualization back into the emptiness from which it initially emerged.

This is important because all of the things you have been visualizing are not substantial entities but are a display of emptiness itself. In other words, when doing the visualizations you see them as the clear appearance of something that does not exist. While apparent, they are not existent. Furthermore, you see that their appearance or vividness in no way contradicts or obstructs their nonexistence. Conversely, their lack of existence in no way obstructs or contradicts their appearance. Thus the culmination of the practice is to dissolve everything back into its fundamental nature and then rest in the experience of that nature.

The completion stage involves dissolution of all conceptual and material forms – that is, everything that can be perceived in the outer world as well as the projections of your inner conceptual mind. First, all the various realms, each with its own kind of suffering, and everything that exists within those realms instantly take the form of

Tara's mandala. Thus the external universe becomes of the same nature as the palace you have been visualizing, and all sentient beings within it become Tara.

Then you think that the external universe and all beings melt into light and dissolve from the outside inward into the vajra circle of protection (*dorje sungkor*). Once they dissolve into the circle of protection, you think that there is no longer anything outside that. Then the circle of protection melts into light and dissolves inward into the palace. At this point there is nothing outside the palace. This completes the outer process of dissolution.

Then the palace, which is the residence or support for you as the deity, melts into light and dissolves into you, at which point there is no longer anything anywhere in the universe outside of you as the deity. You are now the embodiment of everything. Now you dissolve gradually from both the top downward and from the bottom upward into the heart visualization. That is, you dissolve from the lotus and the moon upward and from Amitabha on your crown downward until all that is left is the white lotus and wheel with the seed syllable and mantra garlands.

Then the lotus dissolves into the moon, the moon dissolves into the wheel, the wheel dissolves into the syllables of the mantras, and these dissolve from the outside inward. The outer mantra circle dissolves into the inner circle, and this dissolves into the white syllable TAM. At this point you think that everything in the universe without exception has dissolved into the syllable TAM.

Then the TAM dissolves from the bottom upward. The AH at the base of the letter dissolves into the main part of the letter, which dissolves into the crescent moon. Finally, the crescent dissolves into the circle, and the circle dissolves from the bottom upward until there is just a tiny point of light. Then, continuing to rest your attention one-pointedly on that tiny point of light, you think that it dissolves into nothing whatsoever.

In that way you enter into the experience of the ground of the visualization, which in the liturgy is referred to as clear light. Resting your mind in that without any kind of fabrication or any kind of ideas about it, not attempting to alter what you experience, is the principal practice of the completion stage.

Rest in awareness, effortlessly, neither recollecting the past nor inviting the future, free of all concepts such as good or bad, for as long as you can. You will recall that we began the practice with the mantra OM SHUNYATA JNANA BEDZRA SOBHAWA EMAKO HAM. With this mantra, our starting point was emptiness. Now, in the completion stage, everything dissolves back into that essential emptiness.

If the protection circle, the palace, and the self-visualization are without true existence, then what is the relationship of this insubstantiality to the phenomenal world? Certainly, we are not trying to negate appearances – to say that there should not be appearances. There is nothing wrong with appearances. They are not in themselves an obstacle. It is our confusion about them that is the obstacle. Because of our confused habit of fixating on appearances as being true and real, we cling to them and to our concepts about them and experience suffering. When we realize at the moment they arise that these appearances have no true existence, then appearances will never be a problem or obstacle for us again.

As I mentioned earlier, to understand one situation clearly is to understand them all. If you understand that the mandala, consisting of the palace, the deity, the protection circle, and so on appears real but is empty and insubstantial in terms of its true nature, then this will help you to see phenomenal appearances in the same way. This is because the seeming existence of things is related to the sounds you hear, the forms you see, and your perceptions and thoughts about them, regardless of whether they are outer appearances or the visualizations of the mandala and deity. You create these appearances through hearing, seeing, and mental concepts. If a deity you have visualized with your mind, vision, and hearing has no substantial existence, is this not also true, then, for any other appearance as well? At the same time that there is emptiness, there is appearance. That is the fundamental nature of things.

Consider the tricks of a magician. Through his art, a magician can produce many soldiers with weapons – a big army going to war. People who do not know that this is a trick would see them as real soldiers and feel that they were threatening and dangerous. If the magician caused the soldiers to march in their direction, they would run away in fear. The reason for their fear is that the soldiers seem real to them. But the magician who has produced these appearances would have no fear. He would not run away because he knows that though the soldiers and weapons seem to be real, they do not truly exist. He knows they are mere appearances, depending entirely on his own acts. In the same way, outer appearances have no true existence. Their innate nature is empty and insubstantial. They only exist interdependently.

The reason this realization is so important is that it is through not understanding this truth that we experience tremendous suffering of every kind. Thinking appearances are real and true, we develop attachment and aversion, which are the root of all suffering. To try to rid ourselves of this attachment and aversion directly is very difficult. However, when we begin to understand the true nature of reality, attachment and aversion will be self-liberated. This is the profound skillfulness of the vajrayana path.

There is a story that illustrates this. A novelist once wrote a novel about a mountain. He described it as the most special of mountains because it was loaded with precious stones. He told many stories and details about it, all of them completely fictional. Nevertheless, many people believed that it was a true story. They got carried away and embellished the story with many more details. The story got bigger and better, and the chain continued. We might say it left a trail of collective confusion. This is like our lives, which we adorn with all kinds of fantasies through our fixations. One day someone who had not gotten involved in this tangled web saw that this mountain lacked true existence. He showed them that it literally did not exist. He freed everyone from this great web of confusion. This is like the Dharma.

Consider this: Sound exists because you can hear sound with your sense of hearing. Were there no sound, how would you know hearing exists? And vice versa? What is sound, anyway? One moment it is there, and the next moment it is gone. You cannot say it went here, it went there, or it should be here or there. However, for your conceptual mind that fixates, sounds exist. In addition, not only do sounds exist but categories of sound exist. Because there are categories of sound, there is attachment and aversion.

In reality, though, where does sound truly exist? It does not even exist in the form of the tiniest particle. It is a combination of causes and conditions. It exists interdependently, and therefore lacks true existence. It exists with the aid of hearing. Without the ability to hear and the mind acknowledging that it is hearing something, we would not hear. Moreover, the mind labels sounds. To our conceptual minds, sounds exist in the label and in the appearance, even though they have no true existence. This practice is a profound method for cutting through these conceptual fixations.

Whether one is enlightened or not, one will see appearances. What is seen may not be any different, but the way it is seen is different. When one becomes enlightened, appearances do not disappear into a vacuum that is empty of everything. One sees and at the same time experiences the empty nature.

Emptiness is not a negation of appearance. Out of nonreferential emptiness, form appears without obstruction. Now you can begin to relate to that understanding of emptiness in an experiential way. This is the beginning of wisdom. This wisdom expresses itself as sacred outlook when you re-arise as the deity.

Carrying the Completion Stage into Postmeditation

Having rested in a state of emptiness for as long as you can, at some point a thought is going to arise. While practicing the completion stage, you attempt to recognize the arising of any thought while it is happening. As soon as a thought arises that brings you out of the experience of the basic nature – at that very instant, riding on that thought – you re-arise instantaneously as Tara. In that way, instead of following the thought, you use it as a vehicle for re-identification with Tara. Thus the thought arises out of this nonreferential state into Tara. You do not go through the process of visualization like we did before. You are marked with the syllables OM, AH, and HUNG at the forehead, throat, and heart.

In the postmeditative state your mind appears as Tara. Maintain the conviction that as Tara you will do whatever is beneficial for others. Furthermore, as explained clearly in the lines of the practice text, as Tara you should see that the nature of all objects and sounds in the phenomenal world are insubstantial and lack true existence. They are without any essence as what they appear to be. Though they seem to exist, they are like a mirage. They are like the illusions produced by a magician, which seem to have substance but have no true existence.

From the ultimate point of view, all appearances are illusion-like. In essence they are the play of the wisdom of the deity – the infinite ways in which the wisdom of the deity is displayed and manifested. That means that everything you see – all appearances such as the bodies of yourself and others and the appearances of the inanimate world – are expressions of the body of Tara. Everything you hear is an expression of Tara's mantra. Every thought or memory that arises in your mind is an expression of that mind's basic nature.

Unless we have sacred outlook, we cannot experience things in that way. But by training our minds in this way we gradually develop pure view, so that eventually we can actually experience the essence of the outer world as the display of the wisdom of the deity. Then we will directly see appearances as the wisdom of the deity.

The ultimate nature of all appearances is beyond being good or bad. To impose notions of good and bad on phenomena is to desecrate what they truly are. As the play of the wisdom of the deity, they lack substantiality and are beyond conceptual limitations. Likewise, all sounds are beyond being unpleasant or melodic. To relate to them as if they had such characteristics is to take them to be truly existent. In the same way, thoughts cannot be said to be good or bad. In essence they are nothing other than the display of the wisdom of the deity, expressing the form of that wisdom. It is very beneficial to meditate in this way during postmeditation.

To help you understand, think of the example of space. There are infinite displays of phenomena in the vast expanse of space. There is daylight, darkness, rain, clouds, wind, birds flying, airplanes flying, and so forth. Yet whatever display takes place, the space itself remains unchanged because of its insubstantial and empty nature.

In the same way, the fundamental nature of phenomena is beyond reference point and substantiality. It is referred to as "thatness," the way it is. Whatever arises from this fundamental nature lacks substantiality, but out of our habits of dualistic fixation and attachment, we see it as real, substantial, and permanent. From this fixation we develop concepts of good and bad, pleasant and unpleasant, and so on. This fixation is nothing other than confusion. We do not see what things are fundamentally, and so from that point of view we are confused. We relate to the world on the basis of these illusions, and experience continuous suffering as a result.

Normally, people's habitual fixations are so strong and thick that they fall either into the extreme of believing that appearances really exist or that there is nothing whatsoever. But appearances are like a dream. They are not different from a dream, because in both dream and waking states whatever you experience appears but has no true existence. Whether you have a good dream or a bad dream, what you are experiencing is your attachment and aversion. Likewise, that is what you experience in your interactions with the world.

When you recognize that you are dreaming, that changes everything. If you dream you have walked off a cliff and are falling and falling, you can experience tremendous fear that you will be hurt. On the other hand, if you are able to see that you are just dreaming, then even while you are falling, there would be no fear, and there would be no fear when you hit the ground. What frees you from fear in the dream is waking to the possibility of the empty nature of the experience.

There is nothing better we can do for ourselves than to experience the basic sanity of things – their true nature, empty of any substantial existence. This is the way to truly simplify our lives. If we examine the situation closely, we see that when we are governed by very strong patterns of dualistic fixation and clinging, our lives become very complicated. Because of our fixations we run into all kinds of difficulties.

This is especially evident in countries such as Bhutan, where the people are very superstitious and entertain all kinds of complicated ideas. They think that there is something threatening up the mountain, though they are not quite sure what it might be. Then down in the valley there is something else. If they cross the river or go down a certain path, it is dangerous. They spend their lives trying to appease whatever is out there in order to avert harm. They are under house arrest, so to speak. They cannot move. Not only that, but because it is so real for them, if they move, they actually do get harmed.

I lived there for a number of years and never experienced any of these things. As far as I was concerned, none of it existed, so I was never affected. However, when your mind entertains a fearful idea and strongly fixates on it, what you fear can happen. I saw a great deal of this in South America as well. It is like that in many parts of the world. If you are captive to such a fixation, then you will be harmed. If you are not captive, then there is nothing there. You can go where you want to go and do what you need to do.

If we simplify our lives, we gain tremendous freedom. For example, there were great masters in Tibet who expressed the insubstantiality of true existence not only in the outer world of appearances but with their bodies as well. There were some realized beings whose bodies were transparent. They had no shadow. They lived in a house, but the house had no walls. The sunlight came right through the walls. They would sit or lay in space as if lying on a cushion or bed. The possibilities are limitless. Yet it all starts with beginning to simplify our lives, shedding habitual tendencies and conceptual fixations.

When we understand the fundamental nature of the world and the causes of suffering, it changes how we relate to the world. A great deal of suffering can be eliminated even just by having some intellectual understanding of this. Then, through this kind of practice we can begin to relate to experiences from the point of view of what they are instead of through habitual tendencies and fixations. Ultimately it will free us from getting caught in confusion and obstacles. This is how we carry the completion stage into postmeditation.

Dedication of Merit

Normally, daily practice consists principally of the generation stage, the repetition of the shorter root mantra and the longer long-life mantra, and the completion stage. Then you dedicate the merit. In the Situ Rinpoche version of the practice, the dedication of merit consists of the four-line prayer following the completion stage and the two four-line stanzas of dedication and auspiciousness found on the last page of the practice. In the Jamgön Kongtrul version it consists of the four-line prayer of dedication and auspiciousness found on the last page of the practice.

Going back to the liturgy, in the Situ Rinpoche text it says, "By this virtue, may I swiftly accomplish White Tara, and having done so, may I establish all beings without a single exception in that state." When you say "this virtue," you are thinking primarily of the virtue of the practice, but by implication this also means all the virtue accumulated by yourself and all beings in the past, present, and future. You are dedicating all of that virtue to the speedy accomplishment of White Tara so that you can benefit others.

Here the wish to swiftly accomplish Tara has two meanings. In the ordinary sense, it means receiving the blessings of the deity to the extent that your immediate aims, such as longevity, health, and so forth, are achieved so that you will be able to develop the power and ability to help others. It also has the ultimate significance of fully accomplishing the deity's state, so that your body becomes the same as White Tara's body, your speech becomes the same as her speech, and your mind the same as her mind. That state is perfect awakening, and through this you will be able to bring countless beings to liberation.

Furthermore, "all beings" here is not limited just to the beings we can see, such as humans and animals. It also means all the beings throughout the universe that we cannot see. It includes everyone and excludes no one.

It is worth noting that in order for an enlightened being to be able to liberate someone, there must be some kind of connection, either wholesome or unwholesome, with the person to be benefited. This creates the possibility for the benefit to occur. It does not matter if the connection you have with a being is through having been harmed by them, because even those who have harmed an enlightened being will ultimately become liberated just by virtue of that connection. This is because an enlightened being never gives up on any being, regardless of whether their connection is positive or negative. Thus any kind of connection is the ground for benefit to occur. That is why making a connection is so important.

~

Student: Is there an appropriate time of day or a special time of month to do White Tara practice? Also, should we avoid meat and alcohol as in the Green Tara practice?

Rinpoche: If you are doing it as a daily practice, of course you would do it every day, and because it is a longevity practice, it is best if done in the morning. Ideally you would do it in the morning because your mind is clear and your body is rested, but do not be too rigid about that. If your schedule is such that with work or other considerations you can only fit it into the afternoon, you should not think that you would be better off not doing it at all rather than doing it in the afternoon. Anytime is acceptable, but morning is optimal. Of course, if you are doing a White Tara retreat, you would do three or four sessions each day.

The designation of practices to times of day is usually based on which of the four activities a practice is primarily concerned with. As this is classified as a practice of pacification, it would normally be done in the first half of the morning. Enrichment or increasing is done in the midmorning or late morning. Attraction is done in the early afternoon, and subduing – such as the Mahakala practice – is done in the late afternoon or evening.

Within every month, the day that is specifically associated with Tara practice is the eighth day of the lunar month. We can extend that to the fifteenth day or full-moon day, and the thirtieth day or new-moon day, which are also very special. But the eighth day is particularly associated with both Tara and Medicine Buddha practice.

Though it is not an absolute requirement, it is always a good idea to do the practice before you have had any meat or alcohol that day. It is not as strict a requirement as it is with the Green Tara practice, but you should not for that reason allow yourself to become lax.

Student: If we do White Tara or another practice we feel confidence in for a person who is gravely ill and dying, would the benefit of that carry on into their subsequent lives?

Rinpoche: Yes, and this would be true regardless of what the practice was. In the case of White Tara practice, it is suitable to do it to pray for someone who is gravely ill or even at the point of death. It would continue to benefit them after their passing from this life. This is principally because, as was said, Tara is the mother of all buddhas.

However, if you are asking about custom, it is customary to use the White Tara practice to lengthen life, and it is traditional to use the practices of Chenrezig and Amitabha to pray for someone who is about to die or has died. However, while that is a valid custom in itself, you need not feel that you have to follow it rigidly. If you have greater faith in one deity, or greater familiarity with one practice than another, you can use that deity and practice for all of these various purposes.

Student: Please say a little bit more about how to maintain oneself as the deity in postmeditation.

Rinpoche: After dissolving yourself into emptiness, you re-arise as Tara, and you generate the attitude that you actually are Tara. This means that after you have finished the practice and entered back into your normal daily activities in postmeditation, you try to maintain the outlook of seeing yourself as Tara. In practice, what happens is that you begin postmeditation visualizing yourself as Tara and then, of course, you become very busy. Though you may be doing all sorts of things, you should try periodically from time to time to remind yourself that you are Tara. In that context it is often more of an attitude or an outlook than a visualization. You think of yourself as Tara or you remind yourself of being Tara, but because you are focusing on what you are doing, you cannot always actually visualize a lot of detail.

The Main Practice: The Torma Offering

We have now covered the three stages of the main practice of White Tara – the *kyerim*, the *ngagrim,* and the *dzogrim*. Following the main practice, you can offer torma if you wish.

When you are doing White Tara as a retreat practice, you should offer torma every day. During retreat this is normally done once a day in the afternoon session. Therefore if you are doing two sessions each day, you would offer it in the second of the two, or if you are doing four sessions a day, you would do it in the third of four, depending on how you are scheduling it.

In the torma practice you invite the deities into the space in front of you and offer torma. Having done this, you request them to remain inseparable from whatever images representing the objects of refuge you have on your shrine.

Setting Up, Consecrating, and Offering the Torma

To begin, you set up a white torma. This is round and has a particular shape, and it has certain things attached to it. At best, this refers to an elaborate torma similar to the one used in the White Tara empowerment. If you do not know how to make one of these, another way to do it is to make what is called a *kartor*. *Kartor* means "white torma." This is a smaller and simpler torma made out of dough that is not too difficult to make.[25]

The first important thing to keep in mind is that your torma offering must be free from stains. This means not only that it must be fresh and clean but that it must be pure in the sense that it is made without miserliness – for instance, the kind of miserliness where you feel obligated to offer it but you wish you could use it for something else. It must also be free from the stains of habitual fixations and other shortcomings.

To consecrate the torma, we use the cleansing mantra of the wrathful deity Trowo Dutsi Kyilwa: **OM BEDZRA AMRITA KUNDRALI HANA HANA HUNG PEY.** This purifies the offering on a coarse level. Any defects are purified so that the offering becomes pure, clean, and

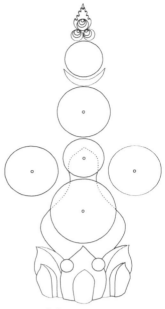

elaborate torma

appealing. This is equivalent to cooking the food you are going to offer to a guest. When you do this practice in an assembly, you will notice that the shrine attendant sprinkles water on the torma with this mantra. When offering torma yourself during solitary retreat, you should also sprinkle clean water on the torma during this mantra. This is more than it appears. The water has been consecrated by this deity's mantra and therefore represents the power of that deity to cleanse the torma.

Furthermore, the offerings should be free of conceptual fixations, such as "This is better than that." To purify conceptual stains, we recite **OM SOBHAWA SHUDHA SARWA DHARMA SOBHAWA SHUDHO HAM.** This eliminates all conceptuality and purifies every-thing into emptiness. Sometimes people think this is some kind of magic spell that somehow physically transforms the offering materials into nothingness, but that is not true. To the contrary, it refers us to the pure nature of all things, which is their empti-ness. It is similar to the *shunyata* mantra you recited previously when you were about to generate yourself as the deity in the devel-

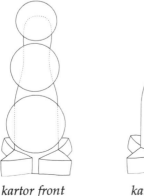

kartor front

kartor back

opment stage of the practice. That mantra was used to remind yourself of the empty nature of all things. The *sobhawa* mantra has much the same meaning.

The function of the mantra is to remind you, the practitioner, of the fact that the offering substance, or anything else for that matter, is empty of inherent existence. The reason this is necessary is that you may have concepts or attitudes about its imperfections. You may think it is too small or is made of an inferior material, or you may have other concepts that cause you to feel that it has limitations. When you purify the torma with the *sobhawa* mantra, what you are purifying is your perception of the torma as imperfect and limited. You are not literally dissolving the substance into nothing. You are dissolving your concept of the substance's reality and therefore its imperfections.

As long as you have not altered your perception of the torma from inherently existent to empty, you cannot consecrate it because you will be limited as to how you physically perceive it. That is why it says at the beginning of the consecration liturgy, "From the state of emptiness." The torma, including its container, arises from emptiness. You think that in front of you, from within this state of emptiness, the plate or bowl that holds the torma itself arises as a huge vessel made of precious materials. This visualization will eliminate any concepts you have about the offering materials.

The torma vessel is vast and inconceivably spacious. It is made of the precious jewels of gods and men, and is unimaginably beautiful. Inside, you visualize the torma initially as three syllables: a white OM on top, a red AH in the middle, and a blue HUNG at the bottom. The meaning of these three syllables is the same as in the self-visualization. They are the embodiment of the blessings, wisdom, knowledge, and noble qualities of the body, speech, and mind of all buddhas and bodhisattvas. You visualize them here so that instead of thinking of the torma as something limited and imperfect, you think of it as perfect and complete.

The white OM dissolves into the red AH, and the AH becomes a white color with a red glow. Then the AH dissolves into the blue HUNG, which dissolves into light of all three colors. As it melts into amrita, it fills the entire offering vessel, which is inconceivably vast and spacious. Finally, the amrita is white, with a slight bluish tinge and it emits red light.

This vast ocean of amrita is perfect in every way. It is an ocean of everything that is desirable. It tastes as good as anything could possibly taste; it looks as good as anything could look; it smells as good as anything could smell. To smell this amrita for even a moment would cause someone's mind to experience immeasurable joy. It is delicious and nutritious beyond compare. Even to have just one drop of it would sustain a being's health, strength, and vitality for many years, and this would be true for anyone. Thus its smell, taste, and nutritive value surpass anything known in this world.

Here we say the mantra OM AH HUNG three or seven times. Customarily we do it three times. As you say this, imagine that the amrita is stirred like milk being churned. It is like stirring with a ladle – the top goes down to the bottom and the bottom comes up to the top. Having done this three times, it is completely mixed. There is a mudra that goes with this, bringing the top to the bottom and the bottom to the top. The food is now ready for the guests.

Having prepared the offering, you then invite the guests. From the TAM in your heart, you radiate light in the ten directions. The light goes to all the pure realms in every direction, inviting Tara in the realm of the Potala in the South, and all the buddhas and bodhisattvas and their retinues. Once invited, they immediately take their place in the sky in front of you as you recite the mantra BEDZRA SAMADZA and do the appropriate mudra. Tara is principal among them, and she is surrounded by all other buddhas and bodhisattvas and their retinues of dakas, dakinis, Dharma protectors, and so on. The mantra BEDZRA SAMADZA means, "Please assemble through the power of your unchanging commitment for the benefit of beings."

Then you say the mantra PEMA KAMALA YA SA TAM, which literally means "A lotus seat for you," with the appropriate mudra. With that mantra and gesture you are offering them white lotus seats and requesting that they be seated just as you would with any guest. Think that they remain at ease in the sky in front of you.

mudra accompanying PEMA KAMALA YA SA TAM

Having welcomed them and offered them seats, you are now ready to serve them. You think that from the seed syllable in your heart there emerge innumerable offering goddesses. All of these are holding smaller vessels of precious materials with which they scoop up from the major vessel some of the ambrosia. An offering goddess goes in front of each recipient of the torma.

Repeating the mantra OM TARE TUTTARE TURE IDAM BALING TA KAKA KAHI KAHI three times, you request Tara to partake of the torma. This mantra ends with the words IDAM BALING TA KAKA KAHI KAHI, which means, "Eat, eat, please eat, please eat this torma." Then, repeating the mantra OM AKARO MUKHAM SARWA DHARMA NAMA DE

NUTPEN NATO TA OM AH HUNG PEY SOHA three times, you invite the buddhas and bodhisattvas and their retinues to partake. The meaning of this mantra is, "Because all things are unborn, AH is the first letter." Although this is often used as a consecration mantra, here it is used as an offering mantra. The offering mudra should be used with both mantras. Then the tongues of each deity take the form of five-pronged vajras. The central or axial prong is hollow like a straw, and they imbibe the torma by sucking it through that tube the way one would drink a soda.

offering mudra

Finally, we make the eight offerings of drinking water, bathing water, flowers, incense, light, perfume, food, and music to Tara and the assemblage of buddhas and bodhisattvas. This is done as explained previously. You emanate the eight main offering goddesses one after the other, each of whom manifests thousands like herself. They make the eight offerings to Tara and the buddhas and bodhisattvas assembled in the sky before you. (*Please refer to the explanation given in the section entitled "Accomplishment of the Deity," beginning on page 49.*)

The Praises and Prayers Requesting Blessings and Siddhi

After these offerings have been made, the emanated offering goddesses make offerings of praises as you focus your mind on and chant the liturgy. First there is one stanza of praise to Tara, and then a stanza of praise to all buddhas and bodhisattvas.

The first section of praises is in connection with the name Tara as manifested in the mantra syllables TARE TUTTARE TURE. First it says, "You are the mother, TARE, who liberates from samsara." She will liberate anyone who turns to her for refuge from the sufferings of samsara. This is not just her name. It is what she is in essence. Whoever turns to Tara with genuine confidence will be liberated. Her ultimate purpose is to free us from cyclic existence.

TUTTARE is another name for Tara, and expresses another aspect of her activities. The text says, "With TUTTARE you free us from the eight dangers." The eight dangers or fears are the temporary relative causes of suffering. Therefore the first praise, with TARE, describes liberation from samsara, or the ultimate fruition. The second, with TUTTARE, describes liberation from relative dangers.

The eight fears or dangers in Tibetan are known as *jikpa gye*. The first is the fear of kings (*gyalpo'i jikpa*). This is danger from harmful authority – for example, a harmful dictator. This is the danger of whatever harm may be directed toward one as the expression of someone's indulgence in whatever power they have. The second fear is fear of fire (*me'i jikpa*). The third is fear of water (*chuyi jikpa*). The fourth is fear of lions (*senge'i jikpa*). The fifth is fear of elephants (*langchen gyi jikpa*). The sixth is fear of poisonous snakes (*dukdrul gyi jigpa*). The seventh is fear of thieves or robbers (*chomkun gyi jikpa*). The eighth is known as fear of cannibals – that is, beings who eat humans (*shaza'i jikpa*). These are not really human beings who eat humans. They are beings in the form of human beings who eat human beings. They resemble human beings but are much bigger. They grab people and swallow them down like a frog eating a bug.

The Tibetan term *jikpa* literally means "fear," but it also means "harm," particularly threatening harm, so it is often translated as "danger." There is an outer and an inner meaning to each danger, so there are eight outer dangers and eight inner dangers. Regarding the outer or relative meaning – in today's world we may face dangers from fire, water, robbers, and those who threaten our lives, but danger from elephants, lions, and poisonous snakes is rare because we now have so much more protection from them than people did in the past. Even though we may not be subject to some of the eight outer dangers in the same way as in the past, however, we are still subject to every one of the eight inner dangers.

The first fear is the fear of kings. The fear of kings has diminished, but is still a considerable danger in some parts of the world. Fear of kings refers specifically to the misuse of the power of a king, but it could refer to anyone who has a great deal of power. In times past, every community, country, or nation was run by kings or warlords. According to history, there were many kings who misused their power, and these were a great cause of fear, danger, and harm to people in all walks of life.

The outer meaning of the fear of kings is quite literal, but its inner meaning is more subtle. It means that one is dependent on others. One's life is controlled by mundane concerns and obligations that, like the powers of a king, keep us from doing what is meaningful. We do not have power over our lives. Our emotions – our neurotic habitual patterns – have power over our lives. Friends and family have a lot of power over our lives. Our worldly concerns and habitual needs pull us away, leaving no time to pursue Dharma practice. That is the inner meaning of the first fear.

In the second fear, even though it is rare to be harmed by physical fire, we are often subject to harm by the fire of anger. Anger and hatred are very serious. The teachings say that one moment of anger can destroy all the merit accumulated in an entire kalpa. Thus anger is more destructive than the worst of fires. It is like a situation where a good seed that has the potential to grow is burned. Its potential benefit is lost.

Third, the risk of harm by water is small, especially if you compare it with the danger of the water of attachment. We are so immersed in the habitual patterns of attachment that we are like a person who is drowning. The power of the water of attachment is pulling us down. It is very difficult to free ourselves from this danger. Even though we know that we need to persevere in the Dharma and exert ourselves completely just as the great yogi Milarepa did, we are drowning in attachment to our bodies and possessions, our families, our friends – attachment to so many things and in so many ways, both coarse and subtle.

Fourth, even if there is no danger from lions, we are continually subject to the harm of lionlike pride. Like the pose of a lion, we have that pose of pride in us. Pride is a serious habitual tendency, and is the source of great deprivation. It deprives us of what is healthy and sensible. When inflated and obscured by the feeling "I know it all" or "I am the best," we are not open to what is to be appreciated and learned or to what gives meaning to life. We cannot settle down and be down to earth. Overwhelmed by the habitual pattern of pride, we lack clarity and compassion.

There are all kinds of pride – national pride, and pride of youth, beauty, family, race, wealth, possessions, fame, or popularity. Regardless of what it is based on, though, we feel, on the basis of this pride, that we are bigger, better, or superior to others. When we are inflated by the habitual pattern of pride, it hinders our ability to see things as they are or to have concern for others. There is a saying that "on the ball of pride the water of knowledge will not settle." If you pour water on a round rock hoping that it will remain, you will be disappointed.

The fifth one is the danger of elephants. How could this apply to us? I haven't seen an elephant since I came to this country except for a couple in a zoo, and they certainly weren't very frightening. But the elephant of ignorance is a serious threat. The elephant is symbolic because he has such a huge body, and yet relatively small eyes and seems to see little. In the same way, what we know compared to what we do not know or know incompletely is very small. Because of our ignorance, we fail to perceive things clearly and directly as they are.

This is very harmful because we fail to do what we must do, and we indulge in what we should not do. We do not understand what to accept and what to reject. Ultimately, this causes great suffering. For example, even a mad elephant could not cause us to be born into the unending suffering of the lower realms. The worst an elephant could do would be to kill us, affecting one life only. But the elephant of ignorance can cause endless births in states of inconceivable suffering.

The sixth one is the danger of snakes. Occasionally a real snake might be threatening, but it is rare to encounter such a risk nowadays. There is, however, a snake that constantly accompanies us and has done so for a very long time. This snake is far more dangerous than even the most poisonous snake. It is the snake of jealousy or envy. This snake causes tremendous harm by producing conflict and dissension between individuals, groups, and even between nations. Jealousy is one of the most harmful habitual tendencies. It causes anger and hatred. It brings great harm to oneself and others and destroys vast stores of merit.

The seventh one is the fear of thieves. Most of us do not have much to steal, and what little we have is not in much danger of being stolen, but there is a big thief that preys upon us constantly and follows us wherever we go like a parasite. It is laziness. It comes in many forms. Sometimes we procrastinate. Sometimes we are distracted. Sometimes we find an excuse instead of going ahead with what we know is beneficial. For many, most of the time that could have been spent on meaningful things is stolen by this thief of laziness. Though it seems harmless at the time, it is one of the most insidious and harmful of habitual patterns, and unlike a thief who may rob you once, it comes back again and again. In fact, laziness is like a notorious criminal. It always knows how to get away with it and there is always a lot of damage.

Because our most effective antidote to laziness is to meditate on impermanence and death as much as possible, it is urgent that we do so. For anyone who is born, death is inevitable and there is no certainty when it will come. If you meditate on this until its reality becomes completely familiar to you, you will have no other thought than to be prepared. With that as a practical basis you will have no trouble keeping constant vigilance over the activities of your body, speech, and mind to overcome this devastating enemy of long standing.

The eighth is the fear of cannibals. Again, this is hardly known nowadays. A long time ago, however, this was a terrifying reality. Some nine hundred years ago there was great fear of cannibals. Sometimes whole villages would be completely destroyed by them. From the Buddhist perspective, the cannibals were eliminated mainly through the enlightened activities of Guru Padmasambhava. It is said in Buddhist teachings that even to this day he is guarding beings from harm by cannibals. Cannibals take that particular form because of the negative and harmful karma they have accumulated, and in this form they destroy many beings.

Not having ever seen, heard of, or been subject to such a thing, you might think that this could not possibly pose much of a threat. This kind of thinking is based on the ignorance of thinking that whatever we do not know or have not seen probably does not exist. But cannibals definitely exist. And even if they do not literally come and gobble us up, we are not free from cannibal-like patterns such as doubt and hesitation.

It is like this: We all have the ability and potential to attain awakening. Not only that, we have the profound methods to bring this about, which have proved their effectiveness time and time again throughout history. Our situation could not be better. Doubt and hesitation are insidious expressions of ignorant mind that constantly deprive us of the confidence to appreciate and take advantage of this. Not only that, we feel deprived. We do not even trust ourselves. Though we are worthy and capable, we think we are not, so we do nothing.

Even for those who sincerely practice Dharma day and night, the habitual pattern of doubt lurks and strikes unexpectedly. As they attempt to embark upon the path properly, it comes uninvited. "Could this really be true? Maybe it's not." Doubt entertains us with many choices. "Maybe it is better to do this," it says, pushing us to act in accord with our habitual tendencies. If anything is foreign to our habitual tendencies, then it pushes us to think something must be wrong with it. Perhaps we think, "Could someone like me do this?" and pull away. It gobbles us up in the sense that it deprives us of the confidence to take advantage of the precious opportunity to attain enlightenment. It robs us of our highest benefit. There is no monstrous being that could be worse than this doubt, this destructive expression of ignorant mind ready to rip us off at any moment.

If we sincerely rely on Tara, she will free us from all of these eight dangers.

Continuing with the praises in the text, it says, "With TURE you protect from all illness." TURE expresses another aspect of the enlightened activities of Tara. Anyone who sincerely and with genuine confidence turns to Tara can become free from any kind of illness.

We are offering praise in accordance with what Tara is. Praise is different from flattery. Praise means you express the good qualities of another, and that you also revere those noble qualities. Here, as an expression of that, you offer not only praises but prostrations to Tara with the words "I praise and bow to the mother, who liberates."

The next stanza is addressed to all the buddhas and bodhisattvas, who with the white light or brilliance of their compassion benefit all sentient beings. The white light refers to the activity of Tara, which is fresh and cool and benefits all beings. Tara is the mother of all buddhas and bodhisattvas, who are the only source of refuge and protection for sentient beings, who without them would have no protectors. Since she has given birth to them, she is inseparable from and is of the same essential nature as them.

In this way we bow down in deep respect to all the buddhas and bodhisattvas.

These praises are not just pretty poetry. They are a sincere expression of appreciation of the actual qualities and activity of Tara and all buddhas and bodhisattvas. During these praises and the prayers that follow, you can play your bell every four lines. [26]

*position of bell and vajra during
praises and supplications*

What follows is a traditional set of stanzas that are chanted in most practices when offering torma. They begin with the sentence "Please accept this torma of offering and generosity." You refer to it as an offering torma because it is offered to all buddhas and bodhisattvas. However, you refer to it as a torma of generosity because you also think that the torma is received by all sentient beings as well, and alleviates their sufferings.

Prayers of request to the assembled deities follow next. With deep respect, we pray that through their enlightened activity they grant all of us practitioners[27] and all those connected to us[28] great prosperity – such as good health, long life, power, affluence, good reputation, and good fortune. "Great prosperity" does not just mean wealth. It means having everything you and other beings need to have a good life. The word that is translated as power actually means something more than "power." It means mastery – to be in control – not subject to being swept into situations where we have no control.

In requesting power, affluence, and good reputation, what we are actually seeking is the capability of benefiting others. In wishing for "good fortune," the word for fortune actually refers to an epoch or time. It means, "May the times we live in be fortunate," not just for ourselves but for everyone. May it be a time of prosperity and welfare and not one of disaster and misery. These are the relative siddhis one aspires to for oneself and others.

On an ultimate level you ask Tara and all the buddhas and bodhisattvas to bestow upon you the ability to benefit others by granting the siddhis of the four activities: pacifying, enriching, magnetizing, and subduing. These are the activities of the enlightened ones that are used to benefit limitless sentient beings. However, to gain and be able to use these abilities, your motivation must be and must remain completely altruistic. Should you attempt to use any of them selfishly, especially magnetizing and subduing, it would be self-destructive.

Finally you request that those with samaya protect you. "Samaya" refers to commitment to the teachings. In this context "those with samaya" refers specifically to beings who are not yet awakened but have a benevolent relationship with the teachings such that they have made the commitment to protect the teachings and the practitioners of the teachings. They are not necessarily human beings. Protectors such as Mahakala, in the presence of the buddhas and bodhisattvas, have promised to appear, assist, and protect in this way. In effect, they have said, "I will take this upon myself as my main duty."

Still speaking to them, you say, "Please assist me in attaining all siddhis." "Siddhi" here refers to the common attainment of pacification, enrichment, longevity, and so forth, as well as the supreme attainment, which is full awakening and the ability therefore to bring other beings to liberation. Though these samaya-bound beings are not yet awakened and therefore cannot grant you these attainments – especially the supreme attainment – they can assist you in gaining these attainments by removing impediments that would otherwise obstruct you.

Then you request protection from untimely death and sickness. The difference between timely death and untimely death is difficult for an ordinary person to see. If someone dies in an accident, it could be untimely or it could be timely, depending upon that person's karma. If it happens suddenly on a relative level, we like to think of it as untimely. However, unless we have insight as to whether or not it involves the ripening of karma, it is not something we can understand. Untimely death means that it could have been prevented if one had applied the proper preventive remedy. In the case of a timely death, it could not have been prevented no matter what one did.

Unfortunately, most deaths are untimely. Many occur because of bad circumstances that could have been prevented had we taken appropriate precautions. We had some control but did not use it. For example, we could have sought medical treatment, done prayers, and/or performed or sponsored meritorious actions that would have prevented death by eliminating the unfavorable circumstances.

In short, in untimely death the potential of life is not reached. A simple example of this might be a car that is designed and manufactured to last a certain number of years or miles. It normally lasts that long, but if the car is damaged or totaled in an accident, it does not reach its potential. That is what we call the untimely demise of the car.

Then you request freedom from döns and obstacles. A dön is often an obstacle related to direction or timing. It is astrological in nature. It has to do with us – our relationship to the elements in our bodies and the elements in the world. Something goes wrong. For example, even if a gift has been given with good intentions, it can still have a negative or harmful effect on us if we are facing in a particular direction or if the sun is in a particular position. The gift can be given with good intentions, and the negative effect has nothing to do with what is given or who gave it to us. Some people may think that such a situation indicates that the gift was given with bad intentions, but it has more to do with timing and our connection to the world. If the same thing had been given to someone else, he or she could probably have enjoyed it without harm. It is a kind of backfiring. Dön can also refer to nonhuman beings who are capricious in their relationship with us and are therefore unreliable, tricky, and generally somewhat destructive.

"Obstacles" refer to situations where something internal or external seems to stand in the way of being able to accomplish something. The term "obstacle" can also refer to human or nonhuman beings who are malicious and for no justifiable reason try to hurt people, obstruct them, and prevent things from going well for them.

Next you request freedom from bad dreams, bad omens, and harmful actions. Bad dreams here does not simply mean "I don't want to have bad dreams that will disturb my sleep." It means "I do not want to have bad dreams that are ominous and indicate that something negative will happen in the future." You are not just asking that the dream not occur. You are also asking that what the dream signifies will not occur.

Bad omens are to be understood in the same way. Bad omens are not superstitions. They are based on something that actually happens. For instance, a wild animal might walk into your house. This is an omen that something is going to happen. You are asking that there be no omen of and therefore nothing that will cause loss or suffering. The implication here is that when the sign or omen is eliminated, then whatever was going to happen is also eliminated.

In requesting freedom from harmful actions, you are aspiring that none of your actions ever become harmful to yourself or others for any reason. Because you are a practitioner, hopefully you will always engage in good actions – but under certain circumstances, even actions done with good intentions can become harmful. Therefore through this request you aspire that none of your actions ever result in any harm whatsoever.

In the last stanza we make general aspirations for the welfare of the world. These are traditional auspicious wishes that good fortune pervade everywhere and that there never be a time when such auspiciousness is not present. They are broad aspirations of well-being everywhere for everyone, free of harm to oneself and others, and free of anything unvirtuous. You do not confine your aspirations just to the spiritual benefit of beings. You make wishes for their overall well-being, praying that both spiritual and physical sustenance flourish. To sum up the whole thing, you say, "Please accomplish all our wishes."

At this point in the chanting you would take the *kartor,* if you have one, outside. It bears mentioning that there are different sorts of tormas you might have, so what you do here varies depending on your situation. If you have a permanent elaborate white torma, you will need a "torma renewal," or what is called in Tibetan a *torsu.* This is placed near the elaborate torma on your shrine before you begin the practice. Traditionally, the *torsu* is a simple round buttered piece of dough, but you can use a cookie or cracker instead if you like. With the torma renewal, you are adding a little bit more to your offering each day so that you are not just offering the same thing again every day. This is not taken out. It stays on your shrine near the permanent elaborate torma.

If you have decided to do the most elaborate setup, then in addition to the elaborate white torma and the torma renewal, you will have a simpler white torma called a *kartor* on your shrine. It would be at this point that you would get up and take out the *kartor.*

If you are a simple yogi – that is, slightly less strict about formal rituals – then you will probably have the elaborate torma and just use a torma renewal. In that case you will not have a separate *kartor* to throw out, and therefore will not have to get up here to take out the torma. Alternatively, if you wish to do it in the simplest possible way, you will not have the elaborate torma and therefore no torma renewal. In that case, you will just have a *kartor,* and you would get up and take that out at this point in the practice.

What follows is the culmination of the prayers. In the versified sections just explained you made many general supplications. Here, in an unversified and therefore more direct and intimate liturgy, you ask Tara to give you what you most want. You say, "Noble Tara, please grant all the supreme and ordinary siddhis." "Supreme siddhi" refers to the attainment of enlightenment, buddhahood completely free of stain or defilement. "Ordinary siddhi" includes whatever you need for practice in order to achieve supreme siddhi – health, material needs, comforts, opportunity, and so on. Therefore the wish for relative siddhi is the wish for all favorable conditions for practicing Dharma.

Though you have requested this earlier, here you emphasize that you especially be protected from present and future obstacles or dangers that create unfavorable conditions for practice. Finally, you request "the supreme gift of a long life of Dharmic activity." To actually accomplish your aims in the Dharma, which is of great benefit to yourself and others, a long life and good health are essential.

This completes the offering of torma.

The Significance of the Torma Offering

For all of this to make sense, you need to understand the significance of the offering of torma. The word *torma* means much more than the literal meaning of the word itself. In Sanskrit, *torma* is *balim*, which means "powerful." In Tibetan, the word *torma* refers to an offering that is subsequently thrown out. Looking at it externally, you are offering a stylized cake or piece of dough. You might think that this is much to do about very little. To the contrary, however, it has great significance, and that is why we have torma offerings in most practices.

If we break the word down into its etymological components, the first syllable, *tor,* literally means "to throw away or dispose of something." Therefore it yields the basic meaning of "disposable" or "cast away." *Tor* signifies the throwing out or getting rid of everything you need to get rid of – all suffering and the causes of suffering – all difficulty, pain, anxiety, and so on. Therefore when you offer a torma and throw it out, what you are really doing is getting rid of everything you need to get rid of.

The second syllable is *ma. Ma* here is more than just a feminine ending to the word, making it a noun. In this case, *ma* means "mother." It means that through offering a torma, you create a situation or relationship with buddhas and bodhisattvas whereby they give you everything you need, just like a mother gives her child food, clothing, a place to live, motherly love, and so on. Thus the word *torma* means more than simply "disposable." It means a process or practice in which you dispose of or get rid of everything that you need to get rid of, and acquire as though given by your mother everything that you need.

It is important to understand this. Otherwise the whole thing can seem like a rather silly cultural tradition. In fact, the practice is the cultivation of an attitude and a process based upon that attitude. As you have seen, the physical offering of that little piece of dough is consecrated. The consecration in essence consists of a complete and dramatic transformation of your attitude toward it and your perception of it. It is your perception of the torma and the attitude you take toward it as well as the motivation with which you offer it to all buddhas and bodhisattvas that transform it from an ordinary piece of edible material into the basis for very effective supplication. Keep this in mind in considering the practice of offering torma, and remember that it is much more than it seems on the surface.

The Apology and Request to the Deities to Remain

Having requested supreme and ordinary siddhi so that you can practice Dharma without obstacle, there follows an apology. This has two parts. During the first, you recite the purification mantra of Vajrasattva three times. This mantra is the most effective way to purify and repair shortcomings and faults in your practice. For it to be effective, it is important to sincerely acknowledge these shortcomings and to have a genuine wish to repair them. Faults in your practice can occur if the offerings are incomplete or impure, if you have recited the mantra incorrectly, if your mind has wandered during practice, if harmful thoughts or thoughts resulting from habitual emotional tendencies have arisen, and so on. These can impair your practice if not purified.

Second, you chant the traditional stanza of apology. The essential point of this is to openly acknowledge the distinct possibility that your practice has been defective. Remember that in referring to whatever was "defective or lacking" you are referring not only to imperfections in the physical materials but to the mental aspect of the practice as well. This is because the most important thing in the presentation of torma is your attitude toward it. This is the basis for consecration, offering, and prayers. Obviously, if you are distracted by thoughts or negative emotions, it will not be as effective as otherwise. It is important to admit that so that it can be rectified.

In effect, what you are doing here is acknowledging that you are still an ignorant sentient being. You may not even remember or be aware of any shortcomings, but you sincerely acknowledge these faults and potential faults so that they can be purified and your practice can become whole or complete. To whom do you direct this apology? "I request the patience of the protectors with this." "Protectors" here refers to the buddhas in their capacity as protectors. Therefore it refers to Tara and all the buddhas and bodhisattvas and other beings who have been invited to receive the torma and your prayers.

Immediately following that, the final part of the torma offering is to request Tara and her assemblage to remain inseparable from the place of practice. This is done when you have what is called a "support." This would be either an image or some other physical basis for veneration of the deity. A support can be anything you would normally put on a shrine as a representation of the Buddha or the Dharma. It can be an image, such as a painting or a statue, but it can also be other things, such as a book of Dharma. It does not necessarily have to be an image of the particular deity whose practice you are doing.

At this point you pray, "Please remain here together with the support for as long as samsara exists." In effect, what you are asking is that for as long as all sentient beings have not yet been liberated, for as long as there are beings who suffer, in order to continue to be active in benefiting and liberating them, please do not depart but remain here inseparable from this support.

Finally, you pray, "remaining here, please bestow freedom from sickness, long life, mastery, and all the best." Freedom from sickness and longevity are obvious. Mastery means control of your situation. "All the best" means that all things go as well as possible in every way for you and for all sentient beings, ultimately leading to supreme siddhi or awakening. For this reason, this expression is usually translated as "supreme siddhi."

It is not the case that buddhas and bodhisattvas will only help sentient beings if asked and will not help if not asked. Nevertheless, what they can do to help is very limited as long as we are not receptive to that help. Therefore what we are essentially doing when we ask them to remain and so on is that we are making ourselves receptive to their help. Though they are impartial, it is necessary to ask because they will be more effective in benefiting someone who asks than someone who does not. As an illustration of this, no matter what kind of liquid you have, if you pour it onto an impermeable rock, it is not going to penetrate it. This is not the liquid's fault. The liquid does not refuse to go into the rock. It is the rock that refuses.

To conclude the request to remain, you recite the mantra, OM SUTRA TIKTRA BEDZRA YE SOHA. This means, "Please remain here in a state of indestructibility." Through the coming together of your sincerity in making these prayers and Tara's excellent qualities, at this point Tara and her assembly of buddhas and bodhisattvas become inseparable from and dissolve into whatever support you have.

As for the other beings, the samaya-bound protectors and so forth, who accompany the buddhas and bodhisattvas and who have also received the torma, you take the attitude that you are a host who has just thrown a party, and you kindly dispatch these guests back to wherever they live. Just as when after a party some of the guests might leave happy and perhaps a little bit intoxicated, they leave with a good attitude and promise to continue to protect you. Through receiving your torma offering, their commitment to the teachings has increased.

Asking the awakened deities to remain has great significance. The places where the Buddha went were blessed by his presence, and we believe to this day, thousands of years later, that these places are in a certain way very different from anywhere else because the Buddha went there, because he taught there, and because he lived there. If you practice there, it seems to go better. The environment itself has somehow been blessed by his presence and activity. It is supportive and uplifting. Somehow the place brings out the best in you.

Not only that but the places where other awakened teachers went and taught the Dharma also seem to carry blessing and power. It is like this because the masters did practices such as this one in that place. Similarly, when we come into contact with an object that was once used by such a master during his practice, it has an inspiring effect on our minds and on our practice. It is also based on this that Buddhists make distinctions between what is called a central region and a borderland. In the Buddhist context this is neither geographic nor ethnocentric. A central region is any place that has been consecrated by the presence of the activity of Dharma. Once that activity is present, we would consider that to be a central region. A borderland is a place where there is no Dharma.

Therefore in order that the place where you practice be consecrated by the deities you have invited to receive torma, you ask them to remain so that they not only benefit you but so that they will continue to benefit everyone else in that place as well. That is why we put so much effort into the creation of supports such as images and books and so on, and so much effort into their consecration.

The Main Practice:
Dedication of Merit and Prayers of Auspiciousness

*A*fter the torma offering you go to the last page of the practice and chant the liturgy for the dedication of merit and auspiciousness. First it says, "By this virtue, may all sentient beings" be benefited in certain specific ways. "This virtue" refers not only to the virtue of this practice but also to all virtue accumulated in the past, present, and future. What follows is a list of the things you want sentient beings to be free of, then a list of what you want sentient beings to have, and finally a line that summarizes it all.

First, "may all sentient beings' wrongdoings, obscurations, faults, downfalls, sickness, and döns be pacified." Of these, the first four – wrongdoings, obscurations, faults, and downfalls – are very much related. "Wrongdoing" refers to what someone does that is wrong. It refers to the action. Although we call it "wrongdoing" or "negative action," it is not necessarily obviously unpleasant to the doer at the time. That is, the person does not necessarily know it is wrong at the time he or she does it. However, because it harms someone else, it creates an imprint in their mind. It will certainly cause them similar suffering in the future, but to a greater extent and many, many times. For example, it is traditionally said that if we kill someone, whether human or animal, we will be killed hundreds and hundreds of times as a result of that single action in future lives, life after life. Therefore the word for wrongdoing in Tibetan is *digpa*, which is also the word for scorpion, meaning "something that is stinging and painful."

Even worse than that, not only does wrongdoing lead to experiences of suffering, it also leads to something much more serious. That is where the second word, "obscuration" (*dribpa*), comes in. Through the imprint of the action whenever we do something that harms someone, we further obscure our own basic nature – our own primordial buddha nature.

The root of all this is what is called here a "fault" (*nyepa*). This means that we have done something that we should not have done. Faults cause us to experience suffering and to become more and more obscured. Finally, this leads to "downfall" (*tungwa*). This means that through negative actions our state degenerates. We fall down and experience lower and lower rebirth, more and more suffering, and so on.

Through the virtue collected in the three times we pray that beings be free of these four things as well as from sickness and döns. In essence, we are aspiring that all sentient beings be free from suffering, from whatever causes suffering, and from whatever causes them to sink further into suffering and confusion. In effect, this is a prayer that sentient beings be free of everything that prevents them from being able to understand or practice the Dharma.

Second, having exhausted all such negative conditions, in their place we pray that beings experience long life, glory, merit, and wisdom and quickly accomplish complete enlightenment. "Glory" has the sense of being victorious over whatever is harmful to oneself and achieving what is virtuous and beneficial to oneself and others. "Merit" is an outgrowth of this and is necessary for wisdom to arise. "Expansion of wisdom" means the revelation of the innate wisdom that abides within the heart of each and every being.

This is a natural consequence of the aspirations we made earlier. When all of the obscurations produced by wrongdoing and so forth are removed, innate wisdom will be revealed. It is like when clouds are driven away by the wind. The moon becomes evident. It does not have to be created. It is already there. It is just revealed.

When innate wisdom is revealed, that being in whom it is revealed becomes fully awakened. This is the state of Tara. Therefore you sum it up by saying, "May they swiftly accomplish the realization of Tara." The prayer has some urgency – that through this merit may sentient beings accomplish the state of Tara swiftly.

Through the power of aspirations and dedications like this, any practice we do will develop into the accumulation of great merit.

Finally we come to the prayer of auspiciousness. Since all buddhas are the same, in a sense we cannot talk about the best buddha. Nevertheless, because it is the function of Amitayus to prolong life and bring about liberation, in a sense we could say that he is the best of buddhas. Thus among all the buddhas, the one renowned as the supreme victor is the Buddha of Limitless Light, Amitayus. Here, when the liturgy refers to Tara as mother, it is not specifically referring to the fact that she is the mother of all buddhas. In this case, mother is used more loosely to mean she is the female aspect of the Buddha Amitayus. You could say that she is the Buddha Amitayus appearing in female form.

The reason we should consider her the female form of Amitayus is that she "definitely bestows deathlessness." She is the mother who can without doubt grant beings the attainment of a state that is free from the conditions of birth and death. Because of that, she is the *Bhagavati*, which means "Buddha." She is that very awareness or knowledge itself of how to place beings in a state of full awakening or deathlessness. Thus she is known by the name *yishin korlo*, or Wish-Fulfilling Wheel.

"May there be the auspiciousness of the awareness-holder, the *Bhagavati*, the Wish-Fulfilling Wheel!" Whenever her name is heard anywhere, there will be auspiciousness everywhere because of the great blessing and inspiration it engenders. Thus this is a prayer of auspiciousness that her activity and her wish-fulfilling name spread everywhere always.

This completes the teachings on the general daily practice of White Tara, the Wish-Fulfilling Wheel. There are more elaborate practices of White Tara. This practice only involves a self-visualization, whereas more elaborate versions have a self-visualization, a frontal visualization, and a vase visualization in the mandala of the deity. However, this is not to say that the present more concise approach is less effective or lacking in any way. By itself it can lead to the experience of perfect awakening.

The Application Practice of the Protection Wheel

We have completed the instructions on the main practice of White Tara, consisting of the development stage, the mantra recitation, and the completion stage. When you have accomplished whatever degree of practice you have committed yourself to, whether it be based on the number of mantra recitations, practicing for a certain length of time, or based on marks and signs of realization, you can then use the practice of the protection wheel that follows to benefit yourself and others.

Ideally, you should complete one or all of these commitments first because that will enable you to successfully perform the applications of the practice. This protection wheel practice is one such application. Although it is permissible to practice it before completing the commitments, its effectiveness would in that case be likely to be very limited. At any rate, I will explain the practice now so that you will understand how to do it when the time comes.

This method is effective in eliminating sudden obstacles or harm to oneself or others. To illustrate how it works, think of a situation where it suddenly starts to rain. You instantly pull out an umbrella to protect yourself from getting wet. Similarly, the protection wheel practice is usually reserved for occasions when there is a special need for it. It is not normally done as a part of daily practice. There is nothing wrong with doing it daily, but it is not necessary.

Here, the protection wheel is entirely different from the circle of protection you visualized as the outer perimeter of the basic visualization throughout the main practice. When you do this practice, you insert it into the main practice right after the dissolution of the visualization before you re-arise as the deity. After dissolution, your mind is resting in a nonconceptual state. When you begin to experience the movement of thought again, instead of re-arising as Tara as you normally do at this point, you immediately go into the protection wheel practice described below.

In an instant, from the state of emptiness, a white wheel with ten spokes appears. Unlike the wheel that you have been visualizing in your heart, this wheel is not flat and it does not have a rim. In fact, it is probably better not to think of it as a wheel at all, because that word is misleading. It might be better to think of its shape as something like some of the satellites we send into space, which are round with various spikes sticking out.

Imagine the hub to be a very, very large sphere of white light. Though it is said to have ten spokes, there are only eight spokes evenly spaced around the horizon. The hub is hollow and round except that the top and bottom are slightly pointed. They are therefore referred to as spokes, making ten spokes altogether. The eight spokes around the horizon are like ribs, and taper to a point. There is no break between them, but there is an arch between them like between the bones on the top of the hand (*or the webbed foot of a duck [Ed.]*). The spokes go all around, and the whole thing would therefore appear circular if viewed from above. Inside the wheel and spokes it is hollow and inconceivably vast and spacious. The wheel is almost invisible because it is spinning very fast. The eight spokes are turning so fast that they are just a white blur, so you can only see it as a tentlike ball. This is the reason why we call it a wheel. It spins clockwise. The upper and lower spokes are turning in place. They are like an axis.

In the center of the protection wheel you appear as White Tara seated on a lotus and moon disk, with all the same adornments as in your visualizations during the main practice. She is marked with the syllables OM, AH, and HUNG at the three places, and in her heart is the mantra wheel with TAM and the long-life and root mantras as before. Amitabha is her crown ornament. You do not visualize the palace now, nor do you visualize the vajra circle of protection you did in the main practice.

Though you will be visualizing the ten syllables of Tara's root mantra in certain places in the external wheel, this is quite different from the visualization you have in your heart. Above you is a large syllable OM, and beneath you is a large syllable HA, both within the protection circle. Slightly in front of the arch at the beginning of each spoke within the protection wheel is a syllable of the root mantra: TA RE TUT TA RE TU RE SO. These syllables are also very large because the size of the wheel and spokes is enormous. None of the syllables are moving, nor are they touching the wheel. The only thing that is moving is the wheel.

From the TAM in your heart brilliant light rays emanate in sequence, one after the other. First you radiate white light, shining like white crystal. Second, the light is yellow, shining like pure gold. Third, the light is red, shining like rubies. Fourth, it is the color of the clear sky at dawn – the blue is very light, almost gray. The fifth is green, shining like emerald. The sixth and last is dark or royal blue, shining like sapphire. In each case the rays go to all the buddhas and bodhisattvas in the ten directions and make immeasurable offerings to them. At the same time, the rays go out toward all beings in the six realms and benefit everyone, endowing them with longevity and everything that could be desired or needed.

The light rays then return, bringing back with them the blessings and protection of all the buddhas and bodhisattvas. As they return, most of the light rays are absorbed back into the seed syllable and wheel in your heart. This causes you to receive and subsequently increase and stabilize the attainments of pacification, enrichment, magnetizing, and subduing.

Not all of the light returns and dissolves into the wheel in your heart, however. Some of the rays remain outside the protection wheel, and progressively form layers or concentric spheres around the protection wheel. First a spherical layer of white crystal light forms one fathom (six feet) outside the tips of the spokes of the protection wheel. This goes completely around the wheel but does not touch it anywhere. Though the layer of white light is light, it is very intense and solid in the sense that it is impassable. Nothing can get through it.

One fathom outside the sphere of white light, a sphere of yellow light is formed. One fathom outside that are formed progressively ruby, light bluish gray, emerald, and sapphire spheres of light, making six protective spheres of light around the protection wheel. As before, the distance between each spherical layer is a fathom, or about six feet. Though they are made of light, the spheres are nevertheless indestructibly hard or tough. They have no fissures or openings of any kind, so there is no possibility that even the slightest breeze can pass through them. They are complete and utter barriers.

The spaces between each concentric spherical layer of light are completely filled with freshly bloomed blue utpala flowers. "Freshly bloomed" means that they are like flowers that open at dawn. They still have dew on them. The flowers are not packed tightly or crushed together. They have some space between them. That space is cool and dewy.

All of the spheres of light are spinning. They spin on the same axis and in the same direction as the protection wheel is spinning. However, the utpala flowers in between them are not spinning. They are not touching the spheres, and are staying in place.

Maintaining that visualization constantly, you recite the ten-syllable root mantra.

The different colored lights embody the four enlightened activities. The white crystal light corresponds to the activity of pacification. It pacifies harm and danger. The yellow-gold colored light corresponds to enriching. It increases merit, wealth, well being, and so on. The ruby-colored light corresponds to magnetizing, through which one gains dignity, power, radiance, and majesty, or becomes magnetizing. The sapphire color corresponds to subduing. This is the wrathful activity of destroying whatever is harmful, such as hatred. The emerald light is a combination of all of the above activities. The bluish gray light is any activity other than the former five.

Nothing can penetrate this multilayered protection wheel. It is indestructible, like an impenetrable force field. No conflict, event, or calamity of any kind can ever violate it or affect it in any way.

To use this practice to benefit others, visualize whoever needs protection below yourself as Tara and within the space of the protection wheel, whether it be an individual, a community, or a nation. To do it for someone with whom you have a special relationship, such as a master of the lineage or your personal teacher, then you should think that they are in their ordinary form in front of you in the middle of all these circles of protection. It is not necessary to visualize them in detail. Simply imagine that they are present in front of you.

This practice is normally inserted into the daily practice. However, when you have accomplished some realization and if there is an urgent need, you can do it immediately on the spot by simply doing the visualizations and reciting the mantra.

At the end of the session you go back to the main text and chant the dissolution of the visualization again. The only difference from the main practice dissolution is that, though you chant the same text, what you dissolve is different. In the main practice you begin by dissolving the vajra protection circle and the crystal palace. This time you dissolve the spinning concentric spheres of different-colored light, the utpala flowers, the spinning protection wheel, and so on. Then you re-arise in the basic form of the deity as in the main practice and do the dedication of merit and the concluding verses on the last page of the practice.

Since this practice is done only when people need extra protection – times when one or more persons are threatened by a specific extreme danger – obviously you must be aware of it beforehand. In addition, for it to be effective, it must be within the limits of your capabilities. Accomplishing at least one of the three practice commitments creates the necessary basis for accomplishing the benefits of the practice. Without it, the practice will have no power. One million recitations of the mantra is the bare minimum, and that is adequate only if you do it properly, with full understanding and sincerity. You also need to have trained in the practice of the circle of protection itself so that you will have a stable visualization when the time comes that it is needed.

~

Student: Do the utpala flowers in the intermediate spaces symbolize coolness and freshness? Do they face a certain way?

Rinpoche: I have not come across any commentaries saying that specifically, but in other practices with similar visualizations they have the qualities of freshness or coolness in the sense that they are fresh because they have not been used, and they are cool because they represent relief from the heat of suffering. It is like that. When I was doing the practice, I felt that all the utpala flowers were facing inward toward me as Tara. They were like a vine growing against a wall, the flowers facing me. It was fresh as if with morning dew. I have never been told what they specifically symbolize.

Gaining the Power to Benefit Beings

It is only after having achieved a certain degree of realization that we will be able to accomplish significant benefit for beings. As mentioned previously, in order to gain accomplishment in the practice of Tara, we must have completed at least one of the three kinds of commitments to practice – through number, time, or lifelong commitment. When a person has accomplished the meaning of the practice, it is said that there are twenty-two different methods through which he or she can benefit others and help them to attain relative and ultimate siddhi.

Therefore it is of supreme importance that we accomplish the meaning of the practice. Without realization, we would not know what these methods were nor how to use them. Not only that but even if we had gained some inkling of what they might be, we would not be able to use them effectively. That is why spending a lot of time immersing oneself in the practice and encouraging others to do so is extremely beneficial. Only if we practice and integrate the practice into our lives can we be the cause of great benefit for others.

Why is this? Think of it this way: It is substance that makes any form meaningful. For example, a blessing cord can have great power. But anyone can say a mantra and tie a knot in a string, and anyone can give you a string to put around your neck. If tying the knot or saying a mantra were all that mattered, then anyone could do it. But there is much more to a blessing cord than that. There are many instances where such a cord has saved someone's life. The cord is just a vehicle through which blessings are received. This is the result of realization – not the power and blessing of mantra by itself. The mantra is a vehicle through which realization is expressed and benefit accomplished.

Thus, giving blessings with the hands and other ways of giving blessing are not just empty ritual gestures or customs. They are methods through which some ultimate or relative benefit is imparted. By itself mantra is not enough.

There is a story that illustrates this. There was once a person who was in solitary retreat. He was a very diligent practitioner. He would leave his cave regularly to gather water and other necessities. His cave was fairly high up on a cliff. One day when he left his cave, the wind was blowing, and it blew one page of a Tibetan text toward him. He picked it up and saw that it was the description of a mantra. It said that if this mantra were recited a certain number times, the practitioner would be able to fly.

Because the wind had fortuitously blown this text right at him, he thought that he must be a destined practitioner of this and that he was very lucky to have found it. What he did not realize was that the text was one page of a longer book, and the mantra that he saw there was an application mantra. Before you do any application mantra, you must always complete the main practice of whatever deity cycle it is drawn from. After completing the main practice, then you can separately practice the application mantra, and on the strength of the main practice there is a chance that it will work. He did not understand this, since it came to him completely out of context. He went back into his cave and started chanting this mantra because he thought it would be very good to be able to fly.

Not knowing it was an extract from a longer practice, he did not know what meditation was supposed to accompany it nor what deity the practice was based on. All he knew was the mantra, so he just sat there and chanted the mantra. He firmly believed that if he said the requisite number of mantras, he would be able to fly. On the day that he finished the recitation, he went to the door of his cave, looked down into the chasm over which he lived, and thought, "I'll see." He jumped, went straight down, and broke his legs.

While he was lying there at the side of the riverbed with broken legs, someone came along and saw him and said, "What happened to you?" He answered, "I was defeated by a text." Therefore it is important to understand that you must do the main practice extensively before you are able to accomplish any applications effectively and actually benefit beings.

Along the same lines, and since we are on this subject, it happens a lot nowadays that people – especially people from the West with no formal connection to Dharma through refuge or teachings and who therefore do not understand the context of vajrayana practice – will come across a book while they are browsing in a bookstore that presents methods of practice drawn from the vajrayana Buddhist tradition. This could include such things as *tummo*, illusory body practice, dream yoga, *powa*, clear light yoga, or something similar. These books talk about how profound these practices are but often neglect to mention that they fit into the context of a larger training and that in order to do them one needs the necessary preliminary stages of practice, empowerments, transmissions, and full instruction. These people buy the book, read it, and start doing the practice. Of course, it does not work because it is taken out of context.

Sometimes I come across one of these people and they will say, "I have been a practitioner for many, many years." When I ask what the person's background of practice is, they will say, "Well, I saw such and such words in such and such a book and that has been the basis of my practice." Now, if this person is developing loving-kindness and compassion, then there may be some benefit. But if their attempt to practice is completely out of context and they do not understand the fundamentals of practice and are simply fixated on a particular method in a book that they happened to read, then they are basically in the same situation as the fellow who jumped out of the cave and broke his legs. That is why it is very important to proceed methodically with your training and to have access to regular instruction from qualified teachers.

Hence, it is substance that is important. To benefit oneself and others, one must of course accomplish the recitation of the mantra a certain number of times, but that should be within the context of the complete practice. The mantra is like an arrow. If you tell someone that an arrow will do this or that, any intelligent person will say, "No, it isn't like that. An arrow doesn't do that – not by itself." The mantra will have a powerful effect only if one's practice is endowed with realization. This occurs not because of the mantra but because of the accumulated power of the practice. It is like an arrow that goes out through the strength of a bow. Conversely, the mantra alone is like a car that is out of gas and will not move. That is why these instructions for practice are so important.

Our situation is like that of someone who needs a house. In the winter it gets cold and we need protection from the cold. We might manage to make it through the summer without a house, but in the winter we need a house and a source of heat. However, if at the beginning of winter we realize that and all of a sudden decide, "I need to build a house right now," our situation would be impossible. We have to spend time going through the whole process of building the house and establishing a heat source in advance so that it will be there when we need it. In the same way, if we really want to benefit others, then we must do the whole practice with the requisite number of mantras first.

Although the long-life mantra is actually White Tara's main mantra, it is not advisable to focus primarily on that in the beginning. You need to first prepare the ground. Therefore in the beginning the root mantra is recited as many times as possible, and the long-life mantra is done one-tenth as many times, in effect using it as a kind of purification. Later your practice will gradually grow and change.

Conclusion

The most important element you need in order for your practice to be effective is proper motivation and confidence. "Proper motivation" means that your intention in doing the practice is grounded in compassion and bodhicitta. Compassion and bodhicitta are the basis from which all other aspects of the practice grow, so a successful practice that leads to benefit for yourself and others depends on this motivation. Without it, a person is like a broken vessel that cannot retain any blessings or benefit.

"Confidence" or "trust" means the heartfelt conviction that the practice will work and that it will bring about the intended benefits. Ideally, of course, you want technical proficiency as well, such as a clear visualization of all of the details of the deity and so on, but your trust in the deity and in the practice is much more important.

When you find that your performance of the practice is not yet technically up to what you would hope, that should not in itself be an obstacle. It is similar to the situation of someone who has put something precious in a locked room that he cannot for the moment unlock. If you have placed something extremely valuable in a locked room, or you know that someone you trust such as a parent or other family member has placed it there, you can be confident that it is there even though you are unable to see it. You know that if you go through whatever process is necessary in order to acquire it, the thing is worthwhile. When you retrieve it from the room, you know that it is yours by birthright. This is an analogy for the attitude that is referred to as "trust" or sometimes as "surrender."

If you practice with that degree of confidence, you will obtain all the benefits associated with the practice. It is most effective if that confidence is directed toward both the deity and the lineage from which the practice comes. You must have the firm conviction that the practice is valid and effective, that the deity's blessings are real, and that if you do the practice, you will definitely accomplish a certain kind of benefit. Then you will do it with diligence, and it is certain that sooner or later you will attain the results of the practice.

Where we run into problems is when we lack that confidence. If you doubt there is any point to the practice – if you think, "Well, maybe this deity is real or maybe it is just made up," or "Maybe this practice works or maybe it is just some kind of cultural thing," and so on, then not much is going to happen. That is so because the fuel that causes a practice to be effective is your faith, and that is obviously absent.

To go back to our analogy, it is as if you are not quite sure if there is anything of value in the room behind the locked door. In that case you would not bother searching for the key because you think that there is probably nothing in there, and even if there were, it probably would not be worth much.

On a deeper level, there is even more to it than that. This is because the process of awakening involves trust in two principal factors, one external and one internal. The external condition consists of what we have been talking about above and will call here "blessing." This is trust in the blessings of the lineage gurus, the blessings of the deity bestowed through practice, and so on. The internal or innate factor is what we call "buddha nature," and this is the essential basis that enables the practice to work. Ultimately, it is to your own basic nature that you must surrender. Not only do you need confidence in the external conditions but you need to believe in your own basic nature in order to go through the discipline of the practice and attain fruition.

When we look at the stories of the great masters and holy beings of the past, we see that in many cases they meditated on a deity for years and years and did not have any vision of the deity or any signs of attainment. Then, when at the culmination of all of those years of intensive practice they finally had a vision of the deity, in many of the stories they complained to the deity, saying, "You haven't been very nice to me, have you? Why did it take you so long to show up?" In all of those stories the deity, whichever one it is, responded in the same way: "I have been inseparable from you from the first day you started to pray to me and meditate on me. However, you have been unable to see me until today because your obscurations, which prevented you from seeing me, had not yet been removed."

When we actually find ourselves practicing, some people find the practice easy. It goes quickly. Other people find it very difficult. The degree of ease or difficulty in a practice is based upon the degree of karmic obscurations that the practice has to carve through to be effective. If you find a practice difficult, it means that the practice is dealing with difficulties that are inherent in your obscurations. This is not true just for the White Tara practice. It is true of any form of spiritual practice in which you might engage.

I hope you will pay serious attention to these instructions and try to remember and take to heart what has been explained. If it is only on paper and not within you, it will not help you to experience the benefits of the instructions and practice. For example, we may see a picture of food and clothing in a book, but a picture cannot help us. In order to experience freedom from hunger and cold, there must be actual food and clothing and we must eat and wear them. In the same way, the better your understanding of the practice, the more effective your practice will be and the better your experiences.

In order to properly enter into the practice, we must have gone through the necessary preliminaries, and must receive the White Tara empowerment and *lung*, which is the transmission of the unbroken lineage of sound, so that we can formally enter into the practice. Having received the empowerment, *lung*, and instructions are not enough, though. We must practice properly and diligently.

Getting the empowerment, *lung*, and instructions is like a farmer getting some land. It requires work for it to bear fruit. It must be cultivated and seeds planted. Then it must be watered, weeded, and worked in many ways. Those who cultivate the land and sow the seeds not only get enough grain for themselves at harvest-time but get enough to share with others. The more effort they make, the more there is for themselves and others. However, those who have land and seeds but do not work the land and plant the seeds will have nothing to eat at harvest-time, either for themselves or for others. They will have a barren field.

Some people try to practice without having received empowerment or *lung*. Without these prerequisites – or if their practice is incomplete – though there may be some blessing, it will not be as effective. And certainly all aspects must be complete in order to attain any kind of realization.

This is illustrated by many stories. For example, there was once a pigeon who lived in the rafters of a building in India more than a thousand years ago. That building was a place where Buddhist scholars came together every day to recite the sutras. Because he had heard the sutras recited constantly, when the pigeon died, he took rebirth as a great scholar, known as Lord Inya. He was so smart that he was able to memorize 990,000 volumes of the Buddha's teachings almost effortlessly. This was a result of having heard the sutras constantly in his past life. Nevertheless, he was totally lacking in realization because he had not received transmission. This demonstrates that without the proper basis, the complete result cannot be attained, though this is not to say that there is no benefit at all.

These are difficult times, and there are many methods for protection. Probably the best of all of them is the practice of White Tara. In saying this I am not referring just to the application practice of the protection wheel but to the practice in general. Even if you just do the main practice daily, it will be very helpful in protecting you and those connected to you. In the best case, of course, you should complete the practice commitment to its full extent. But until that is done, or even if there is no opportunity to do so, if you practice seriously and regularly with devotion, faith, and confidence in Tara, then you will definitely experience the benefits of the practice.

One serious concern I have is that though the West is known for having thousands of experts and educated people, as yet I have heard of very few westerners who have achieved any degree of realization through practice. I hope you will take heed and take these instructions completely to heart. If practiced completely and diligently, this practice of White Tara, the Wish-Fulfilling Wheel, can bring you to complete awakening.

Sponsor's Dedication

My sponsorship of the publication of this book stems from my great devotion to White Tara, the Wish-Fulfilling Wheel. I can attest to the power of her practice from my own remarkable recovery from metastatic breast cancer. I was on the verge of losing my long battle with the disease when White Tara entered my life. Right after starting her practice I was guided to visit a doctor in another part of the country whose protocol for cancer proved to be highly effective. It was Tara at work! Within a few months, the disease had gone into remission and remains so as of this writing.

Words can hardly convey my gratitude to Khenpo Karthar Rinpoche for bestowing on me the teachings and lung for this practice, along with his blessings and those of the lineage.

May this precious jewel of a book enable many others to enter the gate of her practice and through it attain liberation for the benefit of all beings.

Kristin Van Anden
Bearsville, New York
February 2003

1 Sometimes it is taught that there are four lineages of tantra. However, *anuttarayoga* tantra (*naljor la na may pai gyu*) is a subdivision of *yoga* tantra (*naljor gyu*), making three main lineages.

2 The father, mother, and union tantras are contained within *anuttarayoga* tantra. Union tantra is the inseparability of the mother and father tantras.

3 Literally, the word *siddhi* means "attainment." Supreme siddhi is complete awakening. Common siddhis are relative powers such as clairvoyance and longevity. [*Ed.*]

4 Dromtönpa achieved the realization of Tara as a lay practitioner. He had the highest lay precepts, which are known as *tsang chö*, or *gongmai genyen*. When you have the highest lay precepts you are a layperson in form but you have a complete vow of celibacy.

5 Drogön Rechen was an earlier life of the Tai Situpa incarnations. At that time he was not known as Tai Situpa. Drogön Rechen reincarnated again and again. The Tai Situ name came into existence when, as the teacher of one of the Chinese emperors, he was offered the name "Tai Situpa," a Chinese term which denotes high dignity. Since the name Tai Situpa was offered, there have been twelve Situpas.

6 Pomdrakpa Sonam Dorje was the disciple of Rechenpa and the teacher of Karma Pakshi. The subsequent incarnations of Pomdrakpa have not played a significant role in the White Tara lineage.

7 Orgyenpa was very well known as a scholar during his lifetime but did not have any successive reincarnations. This is true of many great teachers. Therefore you will see some names appear within the lineages again and again, whereas there are others who perform great Dharma activities but do not reincarnate successively in this way.

8 Yungtönpa was like Orgyenpa. During his lifetime he played an extremely important role in the lineage, yet there is no history of successive lines of incarnation.

9 The Shamarpa before this is not in this particular transmission lineage.

10 Another thing Bengar Jampal Zangpo is known for is naming a large lake in Tibet as Sky Lake, *Namtso*. In the middle of that lake there is an island. Bengar Jampal Zangpo named the island *Sormodho*, which refers to how small the island is – the size of a fingernail. He did retreat on that island for twelve years. We do not know how he survived. Normally the lake would have frozen and he would have been able to go get provisions. But the lake did not freeze until he became realized.

11 Sangye Nyenpa is also known as the siddha Tashi Paljor. He was the first Sangye Nyenpa incarnation, and played an important role in holding the lineage. The present incarnation is the twelfth Nyenpa tulku. He has completed intensive study at Rumtek

and is now living in the West. Among his numerous incarnations, this was the only one in which he was a lineage holder of the White Tara practice.

12   Karma Chagme was extremely well known, and played an important role in upholding these teachings. But since then, none of his successive incarnations are in the White Tara lineage. Karma Chagme was the tutor of Mingyur Dorje, and when Mingyur Dorje had visions of Amitabha and received teachings from him, it was Karma Chagme who wrote them down. They are known as the "space Dharma" teachings. Karma Chagme also wrote the short Mahakala practice that we do.

13   Tibet has many regions but it was divided into three main ones. Two of them are known as *U* and *Tsang*. There was political unrest between the political leaders of *U* and *Tsang*, and the Karmapa was forced to leave his main seat and wander around with a number of students. Though he was the Karmapa and the holder of the Kagyu lineage in general, he had no opportunity to hold this particular lineage. The political unrest continued after he died, and perhaps because of the unrest the eleventh and twelfth Karmapas died when they were young.

14   Here, when you go for refuge to the Buddha, you are regarding the Buddha not merely as one historical buddha but as all buddhas who have ever in the past, are now, or ever will in the future attain the state of full awakening. Furthermore, you are considering the state of awakening itself to be the trikaya, or three bodies – the dharmakaya, which is the state of awakening itself, and the samboghakaya and nirmanakaya, which are emanated for the benefit of others. Thus in going for refuge to the Buddha you are going for refuge to the trikaya of the past, present, and future.

15   *Chö* also refers to the living Dharma of realization – all of the realizations of the meaning of Dharma that exist in the minds of all who are elevated in having realized the true nature of things.

16   The word for Dharma in Tibetan is *chö*. The literal meaning of *chö* is "to change the course." For example, a person suffering from some illness wishes to have something that will cure his illness. Introducing a change to reverse the course of the illness is the *chö*. The great Buddhist masters Yiknyen and Vasubandu said that the meaning of Dharma is twofold: *Chöpa* (pronounced "chuepa") and *kyöpa* (pronounced "kyuepa"). *Chöpa* means "to change the course or bring about the opposite effect," such as the change or reverse that occurs when one cures the cause of an illness and returns to health. Thus, the course of our defilements is changed on the path, and we become liberated from defilements.

But *chöpa* alone is not the complete definition of Dharma. It is also *kyöpa*, which means "to protect." In this context it means to protect from future recurrences. The twofold benefit of *chöpa* and *kyöpa* are the relative and ultimate effects of Dharma. Vasubandu clearly and frankly stated that the profundity of buddhadharma lies in this fact. Because the Dharma has this twofold benefit of *chöpa* and *kyöpa*, any genuine practice should include both. Certainly, if one could only remove one's sufferings through Dharma but not protect from possible relapse, the benefit would eventually be exhausted and one would fall back into one's defilements and suffering again.

17 *Shunyata* refers to the emptiness of both our phenomenal world and the inner conceptual mind that clings to appearances. The objects that mind clings to are the objects of the five senses: form, feeling, sounds, and so on. That which clings to them is conceptual mind. When we examine this conceptual mind, we begin to see that it does not truly exist. If this clinging mind has no true existence, then form and so on cannot exist. That is because they are interdependent. What clings and that to which it clings exist only in dependence upon one another. Therefore the phenomenal world cannot on its own exist. Both lack true existence. In this way, they are empty and free of reference point altogether.

However, to simply say that they do not exist and are therefore empty is just a thought. You negate existence when you say it is empty, and this is not a complete understanding. Emptiness is not a frightening thing with everything gone and nothing to relate to. Quite the contrary. Because of the truth of emptiness, the play of wisdom can take place. You cannot say that this is primordial wisdom and that is emptiness. You cannot separate that which is and that which is the pearl of that which is. In this way, emptiness and wisdom are inseparable and indestructible. Wisdom sees that the nature of the phenomenal world and mind is empty. The play of wisdom is the expression of emptiness, and since this is the true nature, it is indestructible.

In relating to the concept of emptiness you should not feel a sense of loss. That is not a correct understanding of emptiness. The purpose of bringing the fruition into perspective here is to create an environment free from impure perceptions so that you can generate sacred outlook.

18 *Bedzra* is the Tibetan pronunciation of the Sanskrit word *vajra*, which means "indestructible." [Ed.]

19 The dualistic mind is impure. The nonconceptual mind is pure and unfabricated. Thus, from out of the state of inseparable emptiness and wisdom, the unfabricated mind arises as the sound HUNG.

20 This kind of practice should help you to develop a deeper appreciation of the Buddhist teachings and vajrayana practice in particular. From the HUNG comes a vajra protection circle and from the DRUNG a palace. It is like slicing off one's conceptual fixation. The palace and protection circle lack material existence, and such a view can be difficult because of our habitual fixation. Also, if the DRUNG really exists, how can it become a palace?

21 Making offerings to the buddhas and bodhisattvas and benefiting sentient beings are extremely important as a basis for visualizing oneself as the deity. It is only through the accumulation of merit, expressed here as offerings to the noble ones and as generosity to sentient beings, that one can possibly accomplish one's innate potential and realize the deity. The accumulation of merit is like a vehicle for realizing the deity. Without it, it is impossible to achieve full fruition or awakening.

22 The form kayas (rupakaya) are the samboghakaya and nirmanakaya. These appear for the benefit of sentient beings, and are manifestations of the ultimate nature, or dharmakaya, on a relative plane that can be perceived by and benefit sentient beings.

23   Let me clarify what we mean when we say buddhas benefit beings throughout the three times. When we talk about a time when there is no Dharma and no buddhas, it is in reference to a particular world. According to Buddhist perspective there are many worlds, and if there is no Dharma in a world, then technically you might say that there is no Dharma and no buddhas. Also, when there is degeneration because of the intensity of the defilements of sentient beings, that means that sentient beings' minds have become sickened by the defilements and would not be able to hear teachings even if the buddhas appeared to give them. In both of these cases, however, the buddhas can still benefit beings by taking physical form, although not through teaching the Dharma. It is in this way that the buddhas work for the benefit of beings during the three times without stopping.

24   The Buddhas Vairocana, Akshobhya, Ratnasambhava, Amitabha, and Amoghasiddhi and their consorts are white, blue, yellow, red, and green respectively. [*Ed.*]

25   It is best if you have an actual torma, but if you wish to do the practice before you know how to make a torma, you can offer cookies until you learn.

26   It is traditional in most practices to play the bell at the end of every fourth line during praises, prayers of auspiciousness (*trashis*), and in elaborate stanzas of offerings. The bell is also played at the end of the eight traditional offerings (*argham, padyam,* etc.), when music (*shabda*) is offered. [*Ed.*]

27   In the text the word is actually *naljor*, which has been loosely translated here as "practitioner" so that it will apply to all of us who are doing this practice. However, *naljor* is usually translated as "yogi." *Yogi* is a Sanskrit word meaning "someone who has fully integrated the path." Yogis have an intellectual understanding of the Dharma, and they know how to conduct their body, speech, and mind in their practice. Their knowledge of methods is not something outside themselves that they try to apply to their body, speech, and mind. Their understanding is fully integrated and put into practice, and therefore they can express aspects of enlightened body, speech, and mind. It is only then that it is appropriate for someone to be called a yogi or yogini. I emphasize this because I am concerned that if everyone is called a yogi or yogini, it would be tantamount to calling everyone "lama." This is a misunderstanding that many Indians and Nepalese people have fallen into. They have developed the notion that any Tibetan practitioner they see is a lama.

28   Literally, it says here "retinue." This means those people who are connected to us for whom we wish to pray.

Appendix A

༄༅། །ཀུན་མཁྱེན་ཏའི་སི་ཏུ་བསྟན་པའི་ཉིན་བྱེད་ཀྱིས་མཛད་པའི་
སྒྲོལ་དཀར་རྒྱུན་ཁྱེར་བཞུགས་སོ།

Daily Practice of White Tara

composed by
Kunkhyen Tai Situ Tenpai Nyinje

ༀ༔

ༀ་ས་སྟི༔

OM SOTI

I prostrate to the Lama and to Noble Tara. Here, from the Mother Yoga Tantra's

Drolma Ngön Jung is [the practice called] "The White One Who Ransoms Death." *The deity of activity and consequently "The Green*

Wheel" was taught first, and then the essential instructions for White Tara, "the Wish-Fulfilling Wheel," were given. *These oral*

instructions are in accord with the treatise of Ngawang Drakpa, which are based on these, and emphasize the tradition of Lord Atisha.

This is for those who wish to do this practice in an abbreviated form. *The following is the lineage supplication for the daily practice*

of White Tara:

NAMO GURU ARYA TARA YE
NAMO GURU ARYA TARA YE

DROL MA NGAK GI WANG CHUG SER
To Tara, Ngagi Wangchug, and Serlingpa;

LING PA
to Lord Atisha,

JO WO DROM TÖN CHEN NGA DRE PAI SHAB
Dromtönpa, Chennga, and Drepa;

DAK PO DU KHYEN RAY CHEN
to Gampopa, Dusum Khyenpa, *[Drogön]* Rechen, and

སྤོམ་བྲག་པ། ། ། ། གྲུབ་ཆེན་ཆོས་ཀྱི་བླ་མར་གསོལ་བ་འདེབས། །ཨོ་རྒྱན་པ་དང་རང་

POM DRAK PA   **DRUB CHEN CHÖ KYI LA MAR SOL WA DEB**   **ÖR GEN PA DANG RANG**

Pomdrakpa;   and to the mahasiddha Karma Pakshi I pray.   At the feet of the Victors Orgyenpa, Rangjung

བྱུང་གཡུང་སྟོན་རྒྱལ། །རོལ་རྡོར་མཁའ་སྤྱོད་དབང་པོའི་བཞིན་གཤེགས། །རིག

JUNG YUNG TÖN GYAL   **ROL DOR KHA CHÖ WANG PO DE SHIN SHEK**   **RIK**

[Dorje], and Yungtön*[Dorje Pal]*;   Rolpai Dorje, Khachö Wangpo, and Deshin Shekpa;   Rikpai Raldri,

རལ་དོན་ལྡན་བན་སྐར་གོ་ཤྲི་ཧེ། །ཆོས་གྲགས་རྒྱ་མཚོའི་ཞབས་ལ་གསོལ་བ་འདེབས། །

RAL DÖN DEN BEN GAR GO SHRI JAY   **CHÖ DRAK GYAM TSOI SHAB LA SOL WA DEB**

[Tongwa] Dönden, and Bengar *[Jampal Zangpo]*;   Lord Goshri and Chödrak Gyamtso I pray.   To Sangye

།སངས་རྒྱས་མཉན་པ་མི་བསྐྱོད་དཀོན་མཆོག་འབངས། །དབང་ཕྱུག་རྡོ་རྗེ་ཆོས་དབང་རྣམ

SANG GYE NYEN PA MI KYÖ KÖN CHOG BANG   **WANG CHUG DOR JE CHÖ WANG NAM**

Nyenpa, Mikyo *[Dorje]*, and Könchog Bang;   to Wangchug Dorje, Chökyi Wangchug, and Namdaktsen;

དག་མཚན། །ཀརྨ་ཆགས་མེད་དུལ་མོ་དཔལ་ཆེན་པོ། །བསྟན་པའི་ཉིན་མོར་བྱེད

DAK TSEN   **KAR MA CHAG MAY DUL MO PAL CHEN PO**   **TEN PAI NYIN MOR JAY**

to Karma Chagme, Dulmo *[Chöje]*, and Palchenpo *[Chökyi Döndrup]*;   and to *[Tai Situ]* Tenpai Nyinje I

ལ་གསོལ་བ་འདེབས། །བདུད་འདུལ་རྡོ་རྗེ་པདྨ་ཉིན་བྱེད་དང་། །ཐེག་མཆོག་རྡོ་རྗེ

LA SOL WA DEB   **DÜ DUL DOR JE PE MA NYIN JE DANG**   **TEK CHOG DOR JE**

pray.   To Dudul Dorje and Pema Nyinje Wangpo;   to Tekchog Dorje and Pema Garwang Tsal *[Lodrö*

པདྨ་གར་དབང་རྩལ། །མཁའ་ཁྱབ་རྡོ་རྗེ་པདྨ་དབང་མཆོག་རྒྱལ། །མཁྱེན་བརྩེའི

PE MA GAR WANG TSAL   **KHA KHYAB DOR JE PE MA WANG CHOG GYAL**   **KHYEN TSE'I**

Thaye];   to Khakhyab Dorje and Pema Wangchog Gyal;   and to Khyentse Özer and Rikpe Dorje –

ༀ། ཁྱོད་ཞེར་རིག་པའི་རྡོ་རྗེའི་ཞབས། ཙ་བརྒྱུད་བླ་མ་ཀུན་དངོས་རྗེ་བཙུན

Ö ZER RIK PAI DOR JE'I SHAB **TSA GYU LA MA KUN NGÖ JE TSUN**

To the Noble Lady who embodies all the root and lineage lamas and to those who hold

མ། གང་གི་སྨིན་གྲོལ་བཀའ་བབས་བརྒྱུད་པའི་སྲོལ། རིམ་པ་དྲུག་ལྡན་རྣམས་ལ

MA **GANG GI MIN DROL KA BAB GYU PAI SOL** **RIM PA DRUK DEN NAM LA**

the six traditions of her lineage of ripening, liberation, and dispensation I pray. Bless that I perfect the

གསོལ་བ་འདེབས། བསྐྱེད་སྔགས་རྫོགས་པའི་རིམ་པ་མཐར་ཕྱིན་ཏེ། འཆི་མེད

SOL WA DEB **KYE NGAK DZOK PAI RIM PA TAR CHIN TE** **CHI MAY**

stages of development, mantra, and completion and accomplish the supreme vajra wisdom body of

ཡེ་ཤེས་རྡོ་རྗེའི་སྐུ་མཆོག་འགྲུབ། རྒྱལ་བ་ཀུན་བསྐྱེད་ཡིད་བཞིན་འཁོར་ལོ་དང

YE SHE DOR JEI KU CHOK DRUB **GYAL WA KUN KYE YI SHIN KHOR LO DANG**

deathlessness. May I become inseparable from the Wish-Fulfilling Wheel who gives birth to all the

དབྱེར་མེད་དོན་གཉིས་ལྷུན་གྲུབ་བྱིན་གྱིས་རློབས།།

YER MAY DÖN NYI LHUN DRUB JIN GYI LOB

Victors, and spontaneously accomplish the two benefits.

* * * * *

སངས་རྒྱས་ཆོས་དང་ཚོགས་ཀྱི་མཆོག་རྣམས་ལ། བྱང་ཆུབ་བར་དུ་བདག་ནི་སྐྱབས་སུ

SANG GYE CHÖ DANG TSOK KYI CHOK NAM LA **JANG CHUB BAR DU DAK NI KYAB SU**

I take refuge in the Buddha, the Dharma, and the Sangha until I reach enlightenment. Through the merit

མཆི། བདག་གི་སྦྱིན་སོགས་བགྱིས་པའི་བསོད་ནམས་ཀྱིས། འགྲོ་ལ་ཕན་ཕྱིར

CHI **DAK GI JIN SOK GYI PAI SÖ NAM KYI** **DRO LA PEN CHIR**

of practicing generosity and the other *[paramitas]*, may I attain buddhahood for the benefit of all beings.

སངས་རྒྱས་འགྲུབ་པར་ཤོག །ཞེས་སྐྱབས་འགྲོ་སེམས་བསྐྱེད་དྲུ། །སེམས་ཅན་ཐམས་ཅད

SANG GYE DRUB PAR SHOK

[Three times.] — *Thus go for refuge and generate bodhicitta.*

SEM CHEN TAM CHAY DE WA DANG

May all beings have happiness and the causes

བདེ་བ་དང་བདེ་བའི་རྒྱུ་དང་ལྡན་པར་གྱུར་ཅིག །སྡུག་བསྔལ་དང་སྡུག་བསྔལ་གྱི་རྒྱུ་དང

DE WAI GYU DANG DEN PAR GYUR CHIK   **DUK NGAL DANG DUK NGAL GYI GYU DANG DRAL**

of happiness.   May they be free of suffering and the causes of suffering.   May they never be without

བྲལ་བར་གྱུར་ཅིག །སྡུག་བསྔལ་མེད་པའི་བདེ་བ་དམ་པ་དང་མི་འབྲལ་བར་གྱུར་ཅིག

WAR GYUR CHIK   **DUK NGAL MAY PAI DE WA DAM PA DANG MIN DRAL WAR GYUR CHIK**

that genuine happiness that is free of all suffering.   May they abide in that great impartiality that is

།ཉེ་རིང་ཆགས་སྡང་དང་བྲལ་བའི་བཏང་སྙོམས་ཆེན་པོ་ལ་གནས་པར་གྱུར་ཅིག །ཞེས་ཚད

NYE RING CHAG DANG DANG DRAL WAI TANG NYOM CHEN PO LA NAY PAR GYUR CHIK

free of all attachment and aversion to those near and far.   — *Thus meditate on the Four Immeasurables.*

མེད་བཞི་སྒོམ། ༀ །ༀ་ཤུནྱ་ཏ་ཛྙཱ་ན་བཛྲ་སྭ་བྷཱ་ཝ་ཨེ་མ་ཀོ྅་ཧཾ། ཀྱིས་སྦྱངས

OM SHUNYATA JNANA BEDZRA SOBHAWA EMAKO HAM

OM SHUNYATA JNANA BEDZRA SOBHAWA EMAKO HAM   — *Thus purify.*

།སྟོང་པའི་ངང་ལས་མ་བཅོས་པའི་སེམས་ནང་ཧཱུྃ་གི་སྒྲ་གདངས་ནམ་མཁའ་གང་བ་དང་བཅས་པ

TONG PAI NANG LAY MA CHÖ PAI SEM NANG HUNG GI DRA DANG NAM KHA GANG WA DANG CHE PA LAY

From the state of emptiness arises the uncontrived mind, manifesting as the resonant sound of HUNG,

ལས་རྡོ་རྗེའི་སྲུང་འཁོར་ར་གུར་མེ་དཔུང་འབར་བ་ཡངས་ཤིང་རྒྱ་ཆེ་བར་གྱུར་པའི་དབུས་སུ་དྲུང

DOR JEI SUNG KHOR RA GUR MAY PUNG BAR WA YANG SHING GYA CHE WAR GYUR PAI Ü SU DRUNG

filling all of space.   From this comes an encircling protective vajra fence and tent, blazing with fire.

ༀ།   །ལས་ཟླ་བ་ཆུ་ཤེལ་གྱི་གཞལ་ཡས་ཁང་།   དེའི་དབུས་སུ་བྲྂ་ལས་པད྄

LAY DA WA CHU SHEL GYI SHAL YE KANG   DE'I Ü SU PAM LAY PE MA KAR PO

Within, it is vast and spacious.   In its center appears the letter DRUNG, which becomes an inconceivable watermoon crystal palace.   In the middle of this appears a

དཀར་པོ་སྟོང་བུ་དང་བཅས་པ་རབ་ཏུ་རྒྱས་པའི་སྟེང་དུ་ཨ་ལས་ཟླ་བ་ཉ་གང་བ་རྙོག་པའི་དྲི་མ་དང་

DONG BU DANG CHAY PA RAB TU GYE PAI TENG DU AH LAY DA WA NYA GANG WA NYOK PAI DRI MA DANG

PAM, which becomes a fully blossomed white lotus on a stalk.   Above this appears the letter AH, which

བྲལ་བ་དེའི་སྟེང་དུ་རང་སེམས་ཏྂ་དཀར་པོ་ལས་ཨུཏྤལ་དཀར་པོ་ཏྂ་ཡིག་དཀར་པོས་མཚན་པ།

DRAL WA DE'I TENG DU RANG SEM TAM KAR PO LAY UTPAL KAR PO TAM YIG KAR PÖ TSEN PA

becomes a stainless full moon disk.   On it, my mind, as the white letter TAM, transforms into a white utpala

།དེ་ལས་འོད་འཕྲོས་འཕགས་པ་མཆོད།   །སེམས་ཅན་གྱི་དོན་བྱས།   །སླར་འདུས

DE LAY Ö TRÖ PAK PA CHÖ   SEM CHEN GYI DÖN JAY   LAR DU SHING YONG

flower marked by the white letter TAM.   The TAM radiates light, making offerings to the Noble Ones and

ཤིང་ཡོངས་སུ་གྱུར་པ་ལས་རང་ཉིད་འཕགས་མ་སྒྲོལ་མ་སྐུ་མདོག་ཟླ་བ་ཆུ་ཤེལ་ལྟར་དཀར་ཞིང་

SU GYUR PA LAY RANG NYI PAK MA DROL MA KU DOK DA WA CHU SHEL TAR KAR SHING

benefiting beings.   Returning, *[the TAM and the white utpala flower]* are completely transformed.

འོད་ཟེར་ལྔ་ལྡན་དུ་འཕྲོ་བ་སྒེག་ཅིང་ཆགས་པའི་ཉམས་ཅན་ནུ་འབུར་ཟུང་གིས་མཛེས་པ།

Ö ZER NGA DEN DU TRO WA GEK CHING CHAG PAI NYAM CHEN NU BUR ZUNG GI DZAY PA

I become the Noble Tara.   Her body is white like a watermoon crystal.   It radiates five-colored light.   She

ཞི་བ་ཆེན་པོའི་འཛུམ་ཞལ་ཅན།   དབུ་ལ་སྤྱན་གསུམ་དང་།   ཕྱག་ཞབས་བཞིའི་མཐིལ

SHI WA CHEN PO'I DZUM SHAL CHEN   Ü LA CHEN SUM DANG   CHAG SHAB SHI'I TIL

is graceful and beautiful, with a loving expression and full breasts.   On her face is a profoundly peaceful

དུ་འང་སྨིན་རེ་རེ་སྟེ་ཨེ་ཤེས་ཀྱི་སྤྱན་བདུན་དང་ལྡན་པ།

DU'ANG CHEN RE RE TE YE SHE KYI CHEN DUN DANG DEN PA

smile.   She has three eyes and eyes in the hollows of each palm and the soles of her feet, making seven

ཕྱག་གཡས་པས་མཆོག་སྦྱིན་གྱི

CHAG YAY PAY CHOG JIN GYI

ཕྱག་རྒྱ་དང་།

CHAG GYA DANG

wisdom eyes altogether.

གཡོན་པ་མཐེབ་སྲིན་སྦྱར་བས་ཨུཏྤལ་དཀར་པོ་འདབ་བརྒྱ་སྙན་དྲུང་དུ

YÖN PA TEB SIN JAR WAY UTPAL KAR PO DAB GYA NYEN DRUNG DU

Her right hand is in the mudra of supreme generosity.   At her heart, the

རྒྱས་པའི་ལྱུ་བ་ཐུགས་ཀར་འཛིན་པ

GYE PAI YU WA TUK KAR DZIN PA

thumb and ring finger of her left hand hold the stem of a white utpala flower with one hundred petals, which

མུ་ཏིག་དཀར་པོ་གཙོ་བོར་གྱུར་པའི་རིན་པ་ཆེ་སྣ

MU TIK KAR PO TSO WOR GYUR PAI RIN PA CHE NA

ཚོགས་པའི་དབུ་རྒྱན་སྙན་ཆ་མགུལ་རྒྱན་དོ་ཤལ་སེ་མོ་དོ་དཔུང་རྒྱན་ཕྱག་ཞབས་ཀྱི་གདུབ

TSOK PAI Ü GYEN NYEN CHA GUL GYEN DO SHAL SE MO DO PUNG GYEN CHAG SHAB KYI DUB

blossoms near her ear.   Her crown, earrings, short, medium, and long necklaces, arm bands, bangles,

བུ་སྐེ་རགས་གཡེར་ཁའི་ཕྲེང་བ་དང་བཅས་པ།

BU KE RAK YER KHAI TRENG WA DANG CHAY PA

anklets, and belt encircled with small bells are made of various jewels, but mainly white pearls.   She is

ལྷ་རྫས་ཀྱི་མེ་ཏོག་དུ་མས་མཛེས་པ།

LHA DZAY KYI MAY TOK DU MAY DZAY PA

ལྷ་རྫས་ཀྱི་དར་དཀར་པོའི་སྟོད་གཡོགས་དང་།

LHA DZAY KYI DAR KAR PO'I TÖ YOK DANG

adorned with many celestial flowers.   She wears an upper garment of heavenly white silk and a lower

དབང་པོའི་གཞུ་ལྟ་བུའི་དར་གྱི་སྨད

WANG PO'I SHU TA BU'I DAR GYI MAY

གཡོགས་གསོལ་བ།

YOK SOL WA

garment of rainbow-hued silk.

དབུ་སྐྲ་ལི་བ་ལྡག་པར་བཅིངས་པ།

Ü TRA LI WA TAK PAR CHING PA

Her curly hair is bound in back.

ཞབས་རྡོ་རྗེའི་སྐྱིལ་མོ་ཀྲུང

SHAB DOR JE'I KYIL MO TRUNG

Her legs rest in the vajra posture.

ༀ།

།གིས་བཤུགས་ཤིང་ཟླ་བའི་རྒྱབ་ཡོལ་ཅན་དུ་གྱུར།

GI SHUK SHING DA WAI JAB YOL CHEN DU GYUR
She has a moon as her backdrop.

དེའི་དཔྲལ་བར་ཨོཾ

DE'I TRAL WAR OM
There is a white OM at her forehead, a red

དཀར་པོ།

KAR PO
AH at her throat,

མགྲིན་པར་ཨཱཿདམར་པོ།

DRIN PAR AH MAR PO
and a blue HUNG slightly below her heart.

ཐུགས་ཀའི་ཆ་སྨད་དུ་ཧཱུྃ་སྔོན་པོ།

TUK KA'I CHA MAY DU HUNG NGÖN PO
In the center of her heart on a lotus and

ཐུགས་ཀའི

TUK KA'I

དབུས་སུ་པད་དཀར་དང་ཟླ་བ་ལ་ཏཱཾ་དཀར་པོ།

Ü SU PAY KAR DANG DA WA LA TAM KAR PO
moon is a white TAM.

དེ་ལས་འོད་ཟེར་འཕྲོས་རང་བཞིན་གྱི

DE LAY Ö ZER TRÖ RANG SHIN GYI
It radiates light and invokes the wisdom aspect of Tara from her natural place,

གནས་ནས་བསྐོམ་པ་དང་འདྲ་བའི་ཡེ་ཤེས་པ་སྤྱན་དྲངས།

NAY NAY GOM PA DANG DRA WAI YE SHE PA CHEN DRANG
similar to the *[self-visualized]* meditation.

བཛྲ་སམཱཛཿ

BEDZRA SAMADZA
BEDZRA SAMADZA

ༀབཛྲ་ཨརྒྷཾ་སྭཱ་ཧཱ།

OM BEDZRA ARGHAM SOHA
OM BEDZRA ARGHAM SOHA.

ༀབཛྲ་པཱདྱཾ་སྭཱ་ཧཱ།

OM BEDZRA PADYAM SOHA
OM BEDZRA PADYAM SOHA.

ༀབཛྲ་པུཥྤེ་ཨཱཿཧཱུྃ།

OM BEDZRA PUKPE AH HUNG
OM BEDZRA PUKPE AH HUNG.

ༀབཛྲ

OM BEDZRA
OM BEDZRA

དྷུ་པེ་ཨཱཿཧཱུྃ།

DHUPE AH HUNG
DHUPE AH HUNG.

ༀབཛྲ་ཨཱ་ལོ་ཀེ་ཨཱཿཧཱུྃ།

OM BEDZRA ALOKE AH HUNG
OM BEDZRA ALOKE AH HUNG.

ༀབཛྲ་གནྡྷེ་ཨཱཿཧཱུྃ།

OM BEDZRA GENDHE AH HUNG
OM BEDZRA GENDHE AH HUNG.

ༀབཛྲ་ནེ

OM BEDZRA NE
OM BEDZRA NE

ཝི་དྱེ་ཨཱཿཧཱུྃ།

WIDYE AH HUNG
WIDYE AH HUNG.

ༀབཛྲ་ཤབྡ་ཨཱཿཧཱུྃ།

OM BEDZRA SHABDA AH HUNG
OM BEDZRA SHABDA AH HUNG.

ཛཿཧཱུྃ་བཾ་ཧོཿ གཉིས་སུ་མེད་པར་ཐིམ།

DZA HUNG BAM HO   NYI SU MAY PAR TIM
DZA HUNG BAM HO.   She melts indivisibly into me.

སླར་ཡང་ས་བོན་གྱི་འོད་ཀྱིས་དབང་ལྷ་རིགས་ལྔ་འཁོར་བཅས་སྤྱན་དྲངས།

LAR YANG SA BÖN GYI Ö KYI WANG LHA RIK NGA KHOR CHAY CHEN DRANG

Again, the seed syllable *[radiates]* light, inviting the empowerment deities of the five families and their retinues.

ༀ་པཉྩ་ཀུ།

OM PENTSA KU

OM PENTSA KU

ལ་ས་པ་རི་ཝ་ར་ཨརྒྷཾ་སྭ་ཧཱ།

LA SAPARIWARA ARGHAM SOHA

LA SAPARIWARA ARGHAM SOHA.

ༀ་པཉྩ་ཀུ་ལ་ས་པ་རི་ཝ་ར་པདྱཾ་སྭ་ཧཱ།

OM PENTSA KULA SAPARIWARA PADYAM SOHA

OM PENTSA KULA SAPARIWARA PADYAM SOHA.

ༀ་པཉྩ་ཀུ་ལས

OM PENTSA KULA

OM PENTSA KULA

པ་རི་ཝ་ར་པུཥྤེ་ཨཱཿཧཱུྃ།

SAPARIWARA PUKPE AH HUNG

SAPARIWARA PUKPE AH HUNG.

ༀ་པཉྩ་ཀུ་ལ་ས་པ་རི་ཝ་ར་དྷུ་པེ་ཨཱཿཧཱུྃ།

OM PENTSA KULA SAPARIWARA DHUPE AH HUNG

OM PENTSA KULA SAPARIWARA DHUPE AH HUNG.

ༀ་པཉྩ་ཀུ་ལས

OM PENTSA KULA

OM PENTSA KULA

པ་རི་ཝ་ར་ཨ་ལོ་ཀེ་ཨཱཿཧཱུྃ།

SAPARIWARA ALOKE AH HUNG

SAPARIWARA ALOKE AH HUNG.

ༀ་པཉྩ་ཀུ་ལ་ས་པ་རི་ཝ་ར་གནྡྷེ་ཨཱཿཧཱུྃ།

OM PENTSA KULA SAPARIWARA GENDHE AH HUNG

OM PENTSA KULA SAPARIWARA GENDHE AH HUNG.

ༀ་པཉྩ་ཀུ་ལ

OM PENTSA KULA

OM PENTSA KULA

ས་པ་རི་ཝ་ར་ནཻ་ཝིདྱེ་ཨཱཿཧཱུྃ།

SAPARIWARA NEWIDYE AH HUNG

SAPARIWARA NEWIDYE AH HUNG.

ༀ་པཉྩ་ཀུ་ལ་ས་པ་རི་ཝ་ར་ཤབྡ་ཨཱཿཧཱུྃ།

OM PENTSA KULA SAPARIWARA SHABDA AH HUNG

OM PENTSA KULA SAPARIWARA SHABDA AH HUNG.

སརྦ་ཏ་ཐཱ་ག

SARWA

SARWA

ཏ་ཨ་བྷི་ཥིཉྩ་ཏུ་མཾ།

TATHAGATA ABIKENTSA TU MAM

TATHAGATA ABIKENTSA TU MAM.

[May all the Tathagatas grant me empowerment]

ཞེས་གསོལ་བ་བཏབ་པས་དབང་གི་ལྷ་རྣམས་ཀྱིས།

SHE SOL WA TAB PAY WANG GI LHA NAM KYI

Having supplicated in this way, the empowerment deities utter

ཇི་ལྟར

JI TAR

བལྟམས་པ་ཙམ་གྱིས་ནི།

TAM PA TSAM GYI NI

these words:

ལྷ་རྣམས་ཀྱིས་ནི་ཁྲུས་གསོལ་ལྟར།

LHA NAM KYI NI TRU SOL TAR

"Just as at the time of the *[Buddha's]* birth he received ablution from the devas, in the same

ལྷ་ཡི་ཆུ་ནི་དག

LHA YI CHU NI DAK

ༀ།

|ཁ་ཡིས།

|དེ་བཞིན་བདག་གིས་ཁྲུས་གསོལ་ལོ།

|ༀ་སརྦ་ཏ་ཐཱ

PA YI

DE SHIN DAK GI TRU SOL LO

OM SARWA TATHA

way I bestow *[upon you]* a bath of pure celestial waters."

OM SARWA TATHA

ག་ཏ་ཨ་བྷི་ཀེ་ཀ་ཏ་ས་མ་ཡ་ཤྲི་ཡེ་ཧཱུྃ།

ཞེས་གསུངས་ཞིང་བུམ་པའི་ཆུས་དབང་བསྐུར།

GATA ABIKEKATA SAMAYA SHRIYE HUNG

SHAY SUNG SHING BUM PAI CHU WANG KUR

GATA ABIKEKATA SAMAYA SHRIYE HUNG.

Thus saying, the water in the vase empowers, filling my

[With this mantra the Tathagatas bestow empowerment]

སྐུ་གང་།

དྲི་མ་དག

|ཆུ་ལྷག་མ་ཡར་ལུད་པ་ལས་རིགས་ཀྱི་བདག་པོ་འོད་དཔག

KU GANG

DRI MA DAK

CHU LHAK MA YAR LÜ PA LAY RIK KYI DAK PO Ö PAK

body and purifying stains.

The excess overflows at the top of my head and becomes Amitabha, Lord of

མེད་ཀྱིས་དབུར་བརྒྱན་པར་གྱུར།

སྤྲུལ་པའི་ལྷ་མོ་རྣམས་ཀྱིས་བདག་ཉིད་ལ་མཆོད་པར་མོས་ལ།

MAY KYI UR GYEN PAR JUR

Now imagine that offerings are being

the Family, who becomes my crown ornament.

made to you by emanated goddesses:

ༀ་ཨཱརྱ་ཏཱ་རཱ་ས་པ་རི་ཝཱ་ར་ཨརྒྷཾ་སྭཱ་ཧཱ།

ༀ་ཨཱརྱ་ཏཱ་རཱ་ས་པ་རི་ཝཱ་ར་པདྱཾ་སྭཱ་ཧཱ།

ༀ་ཨཱརྱ་

OM ARYA TARA SAPARIWARA ARGHAM SOHA

OM ARYA TARA SAPARIWARA PADYAM SOHA

OM ARYA

OM ARYA TARA SAPARIWARA ARGHAM SOHA.

OM ARYA TARA SAPARIWARA PADYAM SOHA.

OM ARYA

ཏཱ་རཱ་ས་པ་རི་ཝཱ་ར་པུཥྤེ་ཨཱཿཧཱུྃ།

ༀ་ཨཱརྱ་ཏཱ་རཱ་ས་པ་རི་ཝཱ་ར་དྷཱུ་པེ་ཨཱཿཧཱུྃ།

ༀ་ཨཱརྱ་ཏཱ་རཱ

TARA SAPARIWARA PUKPE AH HUNG

OM ARYA TARA SAPARIWARA DHUPE AH HUNG

OM ARYA TARA

TARA SAPARIWARA PUKPE AH HUNG.

OM ARYA TARA SAPARIWARA DHUPE AH HUNG.

OM ARYA TARA

ས་པ་རི་ཝཱ་ར་ཨཱ་ལོ་ཀེ་ཨཱཿཧཱུྃ།

ༀ་ཨཱརྱ་ཏཱ་རཱ་ས་པ་རི་ཝཱ་ར་གནྡྷེ་ཨཱཿཧཱུྃ།

ༀ་ཨཱརྱ་ཏཱ་རཱ

SAPARIWARA ALOKE AH HUNG

OM ARYA TARA SAPARIWARA GENDHE AH HUNG

OM ARYA TARA

SAPARIWARA ALOKE AH HUNG.

OM ARYA TARA SAPARIWARA GENDHE AH HUNG.

OM ARYA TARA

ཤ་པ་རི་ཝ་ར་ནེ་ཝིདུ་ཨཱཿཧཱུྃ༔

SAPARIWARA NEWIDYE AH HUNG

SAPARIWARA NEWIDYE AH HUNG.

ཨོཾ་ཨཱུ་ར་ཏཱུ་ར་ཤ་པ་རི་ཝ་ར་ཤ་བྡ་ཨཱཿཧཱུྃ༔

OM ARYA TARA SAPARIWARA SHABDA AH HUNG

OM ARYA TARA SAPARIWARA SHABDA AH HUNG. *[Now they sing:]*

༄ལྷ་དང་ལྷ་མིན་ཅོད་པན་གྱིས།

LHA DANG LHA MIN CHÖ PEN GYI

ཞབས་ཀྱི་པད་མོ་ལ་བཏུད་དེ།

SHAB KYI PE MO LA TÜ DE

ཕོངས་པ་ཀུན་ལས

PONG PA KUN LAY

"We pay homage to and praise the mother Tara, who liberates from all misfortune and to whose lotus feet

སྒྲོལ་མཛད་མ།

DROL DZAY MA

སྒྲོལ་མ་ཡུམ་ལ་ཕྱག་འཚལ་བསྟོད།

DROL MA YUM LA CHAG TSAL TÖ

བདགས་པ་ཐུབ་ནི།

RANG GI NYING

even the devas and asuras bow with their crowns." *Now for the [mantra] recitation:* In my heart on a lotus and

སྟེང་གར་པད་ཟླ་བི་སྟེང་དུ་འཁོར་ལོ་དཀར་པོ་ཚིབས་བརྒྱད་མུ་ཁྱུད་དང་བཅས་པའི་ལྟེ་བར་ཏཱཾ།

GAR PE DA'I TENG DU KHOR LO KAR PO TSIB GYAY MU KHYU DANG CHAY PAI TAY WAR TAM

moon is a white wheel with eight spokes and a rim. In its center is TAM, and at the edge *[of the hub]*,

དེའི་མཐར་མདུན་ནས་གཡས་བསྐོར་དུ།

DE'I TAR DUN NAY YAY KOR DU

ཨོཾ་མ་མ་ཨཱུ་ཡུཿཔུཎྱེ་ཛྙཱ་ན་པུཥྚྲིཾ་ཀུ་རུ་ཧཱ

OM MA MA AH YU PUNYE JNANA PUKTRIM KU RU HA

from the front turning clockwise, are OM MA MA AH YU PUNYE JNANA PUKTRIM KU RU HA.

ཚིབས་བརྒྱད་ལ།

TSIB GYAY LA

ཏུ།

TA

རེ།

RE

ཏུཏ།

TUT

ཏུ།

TA

རེ།

RE

ཏུ།

TU

རེ།

RE

སོ།

SO

ཨི་གེ

YI GAY

On the eight spokes are: TA RE TUT TA RE TU RE SO The letters are vivid

རྣམས་མུ་ཏིག་གི་རྡོག་པོ་ལྟར་དཀར་ཧྲམ་མེ་མི་གཡོ་བར་གནས་པ།

NAM MU TIK GI DOK PO TAR KAR HRAM MAY MI YO WAR NAY PA

white like pearl beads, and remain motionless.

དེ་ལས་འོད་འཕྲོས

DE LAY Ö TRÖ

Light radiates from them, making offerings to the Victors

༄༅།   །རྒྱལ་བ་སྲས་བཅས་མཆོད།   སེམས་ཅན་རྣམས་ཀྱི་ཚེ་སྤེལ་བ་སོགས་ཀྱི

GYAL WA SAY CHAY CHÖ   **SEM CHEN NAM KYI TSE PEL WA SOK KYI**

and their sons, and benefiting beings with long life and so forth.   The blessings of

དོན་བྱས།   འཕགས་པ་རྣམས་ཀྱི་བྱིན་རླབས་དང་བརྟན་གཡོ་འཁོར་འདས་ཀྱི་ཚེ་བཅུད

DÖN JAY   **PAK PA NAM KYI JIN LAB DANG TEN YO KHOR DAY KYI TSE CHU**

the Noble Ones and the vital essence and siddhis of the world and beings of samsara and nirvana are

དངོས་གྲུབ་ཐམས་ཅད་འོད་ཟེར་གྱི་རྣམ་པར་དུ   ས་བོན་སྔགས་ཕྲེང་དང་བཅས་པ་ལ

NGÖ DRUB TAM CHAY Ö ZER GYI NAM PAR DU   **SA BÖN NGAK TRENG DANG CHAY PA LA**

collected in the form of light and are absorbed back into the seed syllable and mantra circles, which blaze

ཐིམ་པས་བཀྲག་མདངས་གཟི་བརྗིད་རབ་ཏུ་འབར་ཞིང་འཆི་མེད་ཚེ་ཡི་དངོས་གྲུབ་ཐོབ་པར་གྱུར

TIM PAY TRAK DANG ZI JI RAB TU BAR SHING CHI MAY TSE YI NGÖ DRUB TOB PAR GYUR

brilliantly and majestically.   I receive the siddhi of deathlessness.   *Thus, remaining in one-pointed samadhi, recite*

།ཅེས་པའི་ཏིང་ངེ་འཛིན་ལ་རྩེ་གཅིག་ཏུ་གནས་ནས།   ཨོཾ་ཏཱ་རེ་ཏུཏྟཱ་རེ་ཏུ་རེ་སྭཱ་ཧཱ།   །ཞེས་རྩ་བའི་ཡི་གེ

                                                      OM TARE TUTTARE TURE SOHA

the ten syllables of the root mantra as much as possible: OM TARE TUTTARE TURE SOHA

བཅུ་པ་ཅི་ནུས་བཟླ།   མཐར་ནི   ཨོཾ་ཏཱ་རེ་ཏུཏྟཱ་རེ་ཏུ་རེ་མ་མ་ཨཱ་ཡུཿཔུཎྱེ་ཛྙཱ་ན་པུཥྚིཾ་ཀུ་རུ་སྭཱ་ཧཱ།

OM TARE TUTTARE TURE MAMA AYU PUNYE JNANA PUKTRIM KURU SOHA

Finally,   OM TARE TUTTARE TURE MAMA AYU PUNYE JNANA PUKTRIM KURU SOHA.

།ཞེས་ཚེ་སྒྲུབ་ཚིགས་ཅན་ཡང་བརྒྱ་རྩ་བརྒྱད་རེ་བཟླའོ།   །བསྙེན་པའི་སྐབས་སུ་རྩ་སྔགས་འབུམ་ཚོ་བཅུས་གྲངས་བསྙེན

— Recite this long-life mantra **108 times**.   *When accumulating repetitions, one million recitations of the root mantra is said to be the*

ཐེབས་པ་ཡིན་ལ། ཁྲི་བ་བཟླས་པས་ལས་ཐམས་ཅད་འགྲུབ་པར་བ་ཤད། ཞག་བདུན་ཚམ་ལ་མཚམས་བཅད་ནས

accomplishment of the mantra.   With ten million, it is said that all activities are accomplished.   Even in a retreat of about seven days,

གུས་སྤྲོ་དང་བཅས་ཏེ་བཟླས་པས་ཀྱང་དུས་མིན་གྱི་འཆི་བ་བཟློག་ནུས་པ་སྐྱོབ་ནས་གྲུབ་བོ། །དེ་འང་ཚེ་སྐྲུབ་གཙོ་བོར

if one recites the mantra with devotion and enthusiasm, one will be able to experience reversal of untimely death.   Moreover,

བྱེད་སྐབས་དང་། རྒྱུན་བསྙེན་ལ་སྲགས་སྟེ་ལ་ཚོགས་ཅན་ཉིད་བཟླ་བ་ཡིན་ནོ། དེ་ནས་ཐུན་བསྡུ་བ་ནི།

when focusing on prolonging life and when doing continuous [daily] practice, the long-life mantra is what should be recited.
Now, to conclude the session:

* * * * *

སྣང་སྲིད་ཐམས་ཅད་འཕགས་མ་སྒྲོལ་མའི་དཀྱིལ་འཁོར་དུ་གྱུར། དེ་ཐམས་ཅད་སྲུང་

NANG SI TAM CHAY PAK MA DROL MAI KYIL KHOR DU GYUR   **DE TAM CHAY SUNG**
All phenomenal appearances become the mandala of Noble Tara.   Everything dissolves into the circle of

འཁོར་ལ་ཐིམ། རང་ཉིད་རྟེན་དང་བརྟེན་པར་བཅས་པའང་རིམ་གྱིས་ཐུགས་ཀའི་ཏྂ་ལ

KHOR LA TIM   **RANG NYI TEN DANG TEN PAR CHAY PA'NG RIM GYI TUK KAI TAM LA TIM**
protection.   Gradually the outer world and I dissolve into the TAM in my heart, which gradually dissolves

ཐིམ། དེ་འང་མས་རིམ་གྱིས་འོད་གསལ་དུ་ཞུགས་པར་གྱུར། ཿ སྣར་རང

DE'ANG MAY RIM GYI Ö SAL DU SHUK PAR JUR   **LAR RANG**
from the bottom upward. I rest in clear light.   *[Here the protection meditation may be done.]*   I re-arise in the form

ཉིད་འཕགས་མ་སྒྲོལ་མའི་སྐུར་གྱུར་པའི་གནས་གསུམ་དུ་ཨོཾ་ཨཱཿཧཱུྃ་གིས་མཚན་པར་གྱུར།

NYI PAK MA DROL MAI KUR GYUR PAI NAY SUM DU OM AH HUNG GI TSEN PAR GYUR
of Noble Tara, whose three places are marked with OM, AH, and HUNG.   Ultimately, the appearance and

ༀ༔   །སྣང་གྲགས་ཀྱི་ཆོས་ཐམས་ཅད་དོན་དམ་པར་རང་བཞིན་མེད་པ་སྣང་ཆ་སྒྱུ་མ་ལྟ་

NANG DRAK KYI CHÖ TAM CHAY DÖN DAM PAR RANG SHIN MAY PA NANG CHA GYU MA TA BU

sound of all phenomena have no inherent nature.   Their appearing aspect is illusion-like, and they are

བུ་ཨེ་ཤེས་ལྷའི་ངོ་བོར་རྣམ་པར་དག་གོ །དགེ་བ་འདི་ཡིས་མྱུར་དུ་བདག སྒྲོལ་མ

YE SHE LHA'I NGO WOR NAM PAR DAK GO   GE WA DI YI NYUR DU DAK   DROL MA KAR MO

utterly pure as the essential nature of the wisdom deity.   By this virtue, may I swiftly accomplish White

དཀར་མོ་འགྲུབ་གྱུར་ནས། །འགྲོ་བ་གཅིག་ཀྱང་མ་ལུས་པ། །དེ་ཡིས་ས་ལ་འགོད་པར་

DRUB GYUR NAY   DRO WA CHIK CHANG MA LU PA   DE YI SA LA GÖ PAR SHOK

Tara, and having done so, may I establish all beings without a single exception in that state.

ཞིག །སྟུན་མཆམས་སུ་གཏོར་མ་འབུལ་ན། དཀར་གཏོར་ཕྱོགས་སྒྲིམ་བ་ཤམས་ནས། ༀ་བཛྲ་ཨ་མྲི

Between sessions, when you offer torma,   OM BEDZRA AMRITA KUNDRALI HANA HANA HUNG PAY

set up a white "chok dum" torma, and then: OM BEDZRA AMRITA KUNDRALI HANA HANA HUNG PAY

ཏ་ཀུནྡྲ་ལི་ཧ་ན་ཧ་ན་ཧཱུཾ་ཕཊ། ཀྱིས་བསང་ནས། ༀ་སྭ་བྷཱ་ཝ་ཤུདྡྷཿསརྦ་དྷརྨཿ་སྭ་བྷཱ་ཝ་ཤུདྡྷོ྅ཧཾ

OM SOBHAWA SHUDHA SARWA DHARMA SOBHAWA SHUDHO HAM

– Thus, cleansing.   OM SOBHAWA SHUDHA SARWA DHARMA SOBHAWA SHUDHO HAM   *– Thus, purifying.*

ཀྱིས་སྦྱང་ས། །སྟོང་པའི་ངང་ལས་གཏོར་སྣོད་ཡངས་ཤིང་རྒྱ་ཆེ་བ་རིན་པོ་ཆེ་ལས་གྲུབ་པའི་ནང་

TONG PAI NGANG LAY TOR NÖ YANG SHING GYA CHE WA RIN PO CHE LAY DRUB PAI NANG

From the state of emptiness arises a vast and spacious offering vessel made of jewels.   Within it, OM,

དུ་ༀ་ཨཱཿཧཱུཾ་འོད་དུ་ཞུ་བ་ལས་བྱུང་བའི་གཏོར་མ་འདོད་དགུའི་རྒྱ་མཚོ་ཆེན་པོ་ཁ་དོག་ཇི་རོ་ནས

DU OM AH HUNG Ö DU SHU WA LAY JUNG WAI TOR MA DÖ GU'I GYAM TSO CHEN PO KHA DOK

AH, and HUNG melt into light, from which arises a torma, a great ocean of everything that can be desired of

མཐུ་སྟོབས་ནུས་ཚོགས་པར་གྱུར། ཨོཾ་ཨཱཿཧཱུྃ ལན་གསུམ་མམ་བདུན། རང་གི་སྙིང་གའི

DRI RO NU TU PUN SUM TSOK PAR GYUR   **OM AH HUNG**   **RANG GI NYING GAI**

superlative color, smell, taste, and vitality.   OM AH HUNG   *- Three or seven times.*   Light radiates

ས་བོན་ལས་འོད་འཕྲོས། ལྷོ་ཕྱོགས་པོ་ཏ་ལའི་རི་བོ་ནས་རྗེ་བཙུན་མ་སྒྲོལ་མ་དཀར་མོ་ལ

SA BÖN LAY Ö TRÖ   **LHO CHOK PO TA LA'I RI WO NAY JE TSUN MA DROL MA KAR MO LA**

from the seed syllable in my heart, inviting from the Potala Mountain in the South the noble White Tara,

སངས་རྒྱས་དང་བྱང་ཆུབ་སེམས་དཔའི་ཚོགས་ཐམས་ཅད་ཀྱིས་བསྐོར་བ་བཛྲ་ས་མཱ་ཛཿ

SANG GYE DANG JANG CHUB SEM PA'I TSOK TAM CHAY KYI KOR WA BEDZRA SAMADZA

surrounded by a gathering of all the buddhas and bodhisattvas.   BEDZRA SAMADZA.

པདྨ་ཀ་མ་ལ་ཡ་སྟྭཾ། ལྷ་རྣམས་ཀྱི་ལྗགས་རྡོ་རྗེའི་སྦུ་གུས་དྲངས་ཏེ་གཏོར་མ་གསོལ་བར

PEMA KAMALA YA SA TAM   **LHA NAM KYI JAK DOR JEI BU GU DRANG TE TOR MA SOL WAR**

PEMA KAMALA YA SA TAM.   Drawing it through the opening of their vajra tongues, the deities partake

གྱུར། ཨོཾ་ཏཱ་རེ་ཏུཏྟཱ་རེ་ཏུ་རེ་ཨི་དཾ་བ་ལིང་ཏ་ཁ་ཁ་ཁཱ་ཧི་ཁཱ་ཧི ལན་གསུམ་གྱིས་རྗེ་བཙུན་མ

GYUR   **OM TARE TUTTARE TURE IDAM BALING TA KAKA KAHI KAHI**   *- Repeating this **three times**,*

of the torma: OM TARE TUTTARE TURE IDAM BALING TA KAKA KAHI KAHI   *the torma is offered to Tara.*

དང་། ཨོཾ་ཨ་ཀཱ་རོ་མུ་ཁཾ་སརྦ་དྷརྨ་ཎཱཾ་ཨཱ་དྱ་ནུཏྤན་ན་ཏྭ་ཏ་ཨོཾ་ཨཱཿཧཱུྃ་པྱེ་སྭཱ་ཧཱ། ལན་གསུམ

OM AKARO MUKHAM SARWA DHARMA NAM A DE NUTPEN NATO TA OM AH HUNG PEY SOHA

OM AKARO MUKHAM SARWA DHARMA NAM A DE NUTPEN NATO TA OM AH HUNG PEY SOHA.

གྱིས་འཁོར་ཚོགས་རྣམས་ལ་འབུལ། ཨོཾ་ཨཱརྱ་ཏཱ་ར་ས་པ་རི་ཝཱ་ར་ཨརྒྷཾ་སྭཱ་ཧཱ། ཨོཾ་ཨཱརྱ་ཏཱ་ར

OM ARYA TARA SAPARI WARA ARGHAM SOHA   **OM ARYA TARA**

*- Repeating **three times**, it is offered to her retinue.*   OM ARYA TARA SAPARIWARA ARGHAM SOHA.   OM ARYA TARA

༄༅། །ས་པ་རི་ཝཱ་ར་པཱདྱཾ་སྭཱ་ཧཱ། ཨོཾ་ཨཱརྱ་ཏཱ་རཱ་ས་པ་རི་ཝཱ་ར་པུཥྤེ་ཨཱཿཧཱུྃ། ཨོཾ

SAPARI WARA PADYAM SOHA OM ARYA TARA SAPARI WARA PUKPE AH HUNG OM

SAPARIWARA PADYAM SOHA. OM ARYA TARA SAPARIWARA PUKPE AH HUNG. OM

ཨཱརྱ་ཏཱ་རཱ་ས་པ་རི་ཝཱ་ར་དྷཱུ་པེ་ཨཱཿཧཱུྃ། ཨོཾ་ཨཱརྱ་ཏཱ་རཱ་ས་པ་རི་ཝཱ་ར་ཨཱ་ལོ་ཀེ་ཨཱཿཧཱུྃ། ཨོཾ

ARYA TARA SAPARI WARA DHUPE AH HUNG OM ARYA TARA SAPARI WARA ALOKE AH HUNG OM

ARYA TARA SAPARIWARA DHUPE AH HUNG. OM ARYA TARA SAPARIWARA ALOKE AH HUNG. OM

ཨཱརྱ་ཏཱ་རཱ་ས་པ་རི་ཝཱ་ར་གནྡྷེ་ཨཱཿཧཱུྃ། ཨོཾ་ཨཱརྱ་ཏཱ་རཱ་ས་པ་རི་ཝཱ་ར་ནཻ་ཝི་དྱ་ཨཱཿཧཱུྃ། ཨོཾ་ཨཱརྱ་

ARYA TARA SAPARI WARA GENDHE AH HUNG OM ARYA TARA SAPARI WARA NEWIDYE AH HUNG OM

ARYA TARA SAPARIWARA GENDHE AH HUNG. OM ARYA TARA SAPARIWARA NEWIDYE AH HUNG. OM

ཏཱ་རཱ་ས་པ་རི་ཝཱ་ར་ཤབྡ་ཨཱཿཧཱུྃ། འཁོར་བ་ལས་སྒྲོལ་ཏཱ་རེ་མ། །ཏུཏྟཱ་རེ་ཡིས་

ARYA TARA SAPARI WARA SHABDA AH HUNG KHOR WA LAY DROL TA RE MA TUT TA RE YI

ARYA TARA SAPARIWARA SHABDA AH HUNG. You are the mother, TARE, who liberates from samsara.

འཇིགས་བརྒྱད་སྒྲོལ། །ཏུ་རེས་ན་བ་ཀུན་ལས་སྐྱོབ། །སྒྲོལ་མ་ལ་ནི་ཕྱག་འཚལ་

JIK GYAY DROL TURE NA WA KUN LAY KYOB DROL MA LA NI CHAG TSAL

With TUTTARE you free us from the eight fears. With TURE you protect from all illness. I praise and

བསྟོད། །གང་གི་ཐུགས་རྗེའི་འོད་དཀར་གྱིས། །མ་ལུས་འགྲོ་བའི་དོན་མཛད་ཅིང་།

TÖ GANG GI TUK JE'I Ö KAR GYI MA LU DRO WAI DÖN DZAY CHING

bow to the mother, who liberates. With the white light of compassion, you benefit all sentient beings

།མགོན་མེད་རྣམས་ཀྱི་མགོན་དང་སྐྱབས། །རྒྱལ་བ་སྲས་དང་བཅས་ལ་འདུད།

GÖN MAY NAM KYI GÖN DANG KYOB GYAL WA SAY DANG CHAY LA DÜ

without exception. You are the protectors and refuge for those without protection. To you, the victors

ཨ༷མཆོད་སྦྱིན་གཏོར་མ་འདི་བཞེས་ལ།

CHÖ JIN TOR MA DI SHAY LA

and your sons, I bow.   Please accept this torma of offering and generosity.

རྣལ་འབྱོར་བདག་ཅག་འཁོར་བཅས་ལ།

NAL JOR DAK CHAG KHOR CHAY LA

May we practitioners and

ནད་མེད་ཚེ་དང་དབང་ཕྱུག་དང་།

NAY MAY TSE DANG WANG CHUK DANG

all those connected to us have great prosperity –

དཔལ་དང་གྲགས་དང་སྐལ་པ་བཟང་།

PAL DANG DRAK DANG KAL PA ZANG

such as good health, long life, power, affluence, and good

ལོངས

LONG

སྤྱོད་རྒྱ་ཆེན་ཀུན་ཐོབ་ཅིང་།

CHÖ GYA CHEN KUN TOB CHING

reputation, and may these be fortunate times.

ཞི་དང་རྒྱས་ལ་སོགས་པ་ཡི།

SHI DANG GYE LA SOK PA YI

Please bestow on me the siddhi of the four activities of

ལས་ཀྱི་དངོས་གྲུབ

LAY KYI NGÖ DRUB

བདག་ལ་སྩོལ།

DAK LA TSOL

pacification, increase, and so on.

དམ་ཚིག་ཅན་གྱིས་བདག་ལ་སྲུངས།

DAM TSIK CHEN GYI DAK LA SUNG

You with samaya, please protect me.

དངོས་གྲུབ་ཀུན་གྱི་སྟོངས

NGÖ DRUB KUN GYI TONG

Please assist me in attaining

གྲོགས་མཛོད།

DROK DZÖ

all siddhis.

དུས་མིན་འཆི་དང་ནད་རྣམས་དང་།

DU MIN CHI DANG NAY NAM DANG

Please eliminate untimely death, sickness, döns, and obstacles.

གདོན་དང་བགེགས་རྣམས

DÖN DANG GEK NAM

Please eliminate bad

མེད་པར་མཛོད།

MAY PAR DZÖ

dreams, bad omens, and harmful actions.

རྨི་ལམ་ངན་དང་མཚན་མ་ངན

MI LAM NGEN DANG TSEN MA NGEN

Please promote happiness and good harvests in this world,

བྱ་བྱེད་ངན་པ་མེད་པར་མཛོད།

JA JAY NGEN PA MAY PAR DZÖ

འཇིག་རྟེན་བདེ་ཞིང་ལོ་ལེགས་དང་།

JIK TEN DE SHING LO LEK DANG

flourishing crops and the spread of Dharma, well-being and prosperity of every kind, and the accomplish-

འབྲུ་རྣམས་འཕེལ་ཞིང་ཆོས་འཕེལ་བ།

DRU NAM PEL SHING CHÖ PEL WA

ༀ༔   །བདེ་ལེགས་ཕུན་སུམ་ཚོགས་པ་དང་།   །ཡིད་ལ་འདོད་པ་ཀུན་འགྲུབ་མཛོད།

DE LEK PUN SUM TSOK PA DANG   **YI LA DÖ PA KUN DRUB DZÖ**

ment of all our wishes.   Noble Tara, please bestow on me all the supreme and ordinary

།འཕགས་མ་སྒྲོལ་མས་བདག་ལ་མཆོག་ཐུན་མོང་གི་དངོས་གྲུབ་མ་ལུས་པ་སྩོལ་བ་དང་།

PAK MA DROL MAY DAK LA CHOG TUN MONG GI NGÖ DRUB MA LU PA TSOL WA DANG

siddhis without exception.   Especially, please protect me from present and future dangers.

ཁྱད་པར་དུ་འཕྲལ་ཡུན་གྱི་འཇིགས་པ་ལས་སྐྱོབ་ཅིང་།   ཆོས་སྤྱོད་བཞིན་ཡུན་རིང་དུ

KHYAY PAR DU TRAL YUN GYI JIK PA LAY KYOB CHING   **CHÖ CHÖ SHIN YUN RING DU**

Please grant me the supreme gift of a long life of Dharmic activity.

འཚོ་བའི་མཆོག་སྦྱིན་པར་མཛད་དུ་གསོལ།   ཨེ་གི་བཀུར་ལན་གསུམ་དང་།   མ་འབྱོར་པ

TSO WAI CHOG JIN PAR DZAY DO SOL   **MA JOR PA**

*Recite the 100-syllable mantra **three times**.*   I pray that the protectors

དང་ཉམས་པ་དང་།   །གང་ཡང་བདག་རྨོངས་བློ་ཡིས་ནི།   །བགྱིས་པ་དང་ནི་བགྱིད

DANG NYAM PA DANG   **GANG YANG DAK MONG LO YI NI**   **GYI PA DANG NI GYI**

will be patient with me for whatever I did or caused others to do that was defective or lacking through

སྩལ་བ།   །དེ་ཀུན་མགོན་པོས་བཟོད་པར་མཛོད།   ཀྱིས་ནོངས་པ་བཤགས།   །འདིར་ནི

TSAL WA   **DE KUN GÖN PÖ ZÖ PAR DZÖ**   **DIR NI**

any kind of bewilderment.   – *Thus, faults are confessed.*

རྟེན་དང་ལྷན་ཅིག་ཏུ།   །འཁོར་བ་སྲིད་དུ་བཞུགས་ནས་ཀྱང་།   །ནད་མེད་ཚེ་དང་

TEN DANG LHEN CHIK TU   **KHOR WA SI DU SHUK NAY KYANG**   **NAY MAY TSE DANG**

Please remain here together with the support for as long as samsara exists and, remaining here, please

WANG CHUK DANG   **CHOK NAM LEK PAR TSAL DU SOL**   **OM SUTRA TIKTRA BEDZRA**

bestow freedom from sickness, long life, mastery, and supreme siddhi.   OM SUTRA TIKTRA BEDZRA

YE SOHA

YE SOHA.   *– Thus, the torma guests are requested to stay in the support.   Do aspiration prayers and prayers of auspiciousness.*

If you wish to meditate on the wheel of protection, then after dissolving the self-visualization and before arising again in the body of union as set forth above:

TONG PAI NGANG LAY KAY CHIK GI KHOR LO KAR PO TSIB CHU GUR TAB SU NAY SHING MI

Instantly, from the state of emptiness arises a white wheel, like a tent with ten spokes, turning swiftly and

NGÖN PAR NYUR DU KHOR WAI TE WA DUM PO YANG PAI NANG DU RANG NYI PAK MA DROL

invisibly.   Within its round and spacious center I appear clearly as the Noble Tara, the Wish-Fulfilling

MA YI SHIN KHOR LO GYEN DANG CHA LUK YONG SU DZOK PAR SAL WAI TUK KAR KHOR LO

Wheel, completely perfect in ornament and attire.   In my heart is the *[mantra]* wheel with its syllables.

YIK DRU DANG CHAY PA   **RANG NYI KYI TENG DU OM**   **OK TU HA**   **TSIB KYI TSA WA**

Above me is OM,   and below is HA.   Within the hollow area of each spoke's joint, from the front

ༀཿ   ཁྲུབས་སྟོང་གི་ཐབ་ཀྱི་ནང་དུ་མདུན་ནས་གཡས་སྐོར་དུ་ཡི་གེ་བརྒྱད་བཙས་ཡིག

BUB TONG GI TAY KYI NANG DU DUN NAY YAY KOR DU YI GE GYAY CHAY

clockwise, are the eight *[remaining]* syllables whose letters are white.   From the seed

འབྲུ་རྣམས་དཀར་པོ།   རང་གི་ཐུགས་ཀའི་ས་བོན་ལས་འོད་ཟེར་དཀར་པོ་ཤེལ་ལྟ་བུ

YIK DRU NAM KAR PO   RANG GI TUK KAI SA BÖN LAY Ö ZER KAR PO SHEL TA BU

syllable in my heart, white crystal-like light radiates.   Then golden yellow [light],   then ruby red [light],

སེར་པོ་གསེར་ལྟ་བུ།   དམར་པོ་པདྨ་རཱ་ག་ལྟ་བུ།   ལྗགས་ཁ་ཏོ་རེངས་ཀྱི་གནས་ལྟ་བུ

SER PO SER TA BU   MAR PO PE MA RA GA TA BU   CHAG KHA TO RENG KYI NAM TA BU

then metallic blue [light] like the sky at dawn,   then emerald green [light],   and then sapphire deep blue

ལྗང་ཁུ་མ་ཀནྡྲ་ལྟ་བུ།   མཆིན་ཁ་ཨིནྡྲ་ནཱི་ལ་ལྟ་བུ་རྣམས་རིམ་པར་སྤྲོས།   སེམས་ཅན

JANG KHU MA GAY TA BU   CHIN KHA INDRA NI LA TA BU NAM RIM PAR TRÖ   SEM CHEN

[light] radiate in succession, benefiting sentient beings and making offerings to the Victors.   The blessings

གྱི་དོན་བྱས།   རྒྱལ་བ་རྣམས་མཆོད།   ཕྱོགས་བཅུའི་རྒྱལ་བ་རྣམས་ཀྱི་བྱིན་རླབས

GYI DÖN JAY   GYAL WA NAM CHÖ   CHOK CHU'I GYAL WA NAM KYI JIN LAB

of the Victors of the ten directions come back successively in the form of white, yellow, red, blue, green, and

འོད་ཟེར་དཀར་སེར་དམར་སྔོ་ལྗང་མཐིང་གི་རྣམ་པར་རིམ་པར་བྱོན།   རང་གི་ཐུགས་ཀའི

Ö ZER KAR SER MAR NGO JANG TING GI NAM PAR RIM PAR JÖN   RANG GI TUK KAI

deep blue light.   Dissolving into the wheel in my heart, the siddhis of the various activities of pacification,

འཁོར་ལོ་ལ་ཐིམ་པས།   ཞི་རྒྱས་དབང་དྲག་ལས་སྣ་ཚོགས་པའི་དངོས་གྲུབ་ཐོབ་ཅིང་བརྟན

KHOR LO LA TIM PAY   SHI GYAY WANG DRAK LAY NA TSOK PAI NGÖ DRUB TOB CHING TEN

enriching, empowering, and subduing are attained and stabilized.   The remaining light forms layers,

པར་བྱས།   འོད་ལྷག་མ་རྣམས་འཁོར་ལོའི་གུར་ཁང་གི་ཕྱི་ནས་འདོམ་གང་ཙམ་ནས་འོད

PAR JAY   Ö LHAK MA NAM KHOR LO'I GUR KANG GI CHI NAY DOM GANG TSAM NAY Ö

[beginning at] about six feet from the outer perimeter of the wheel.   There is a pavilion of white light.

དཀར་པོའི་གུར་ཁང་།   དེའི་ཕྱིར་སེར་པོ།   དེའི་ཕྱིར་དམར་པོ།   དེའི་ཕྱིར

KAR PO'I GUR KHANG   DE'I CHIR SER PO   DE'I CHIR MAR PO   DE'I CHIR

Outside that is a pavilion of yellow light.   Outside that is a pavilion of red light.   Outside that is a pavilion

ལྗགས་ཁ།   དེའི་ཕྱིར་ལྗང་ཁུ།   དེའི་ཕྱིར་འོད་མཆིན་ཁའི་གུར་ཁང་རྣམས་ཀྱང

CHAG KHA   DE'I CHIR JANG KHU   DE'I CHIR Ö CHIN KHA'I GUR KHANG NAM KYANG

of metallic blue light.   Outside that is a pavilion of green light.   And outside that is a pavilion of deep blue

འདོམ་རེའི་བར་ཐག་ཅན།   སྟེང་འོག་ཕྱོགས་མཚམས་ཀུན་ཏུ་འཁོར་བ་བཟླུམ་པོའི་རྣམ་པ

DOM RE'I BAR TAK CHEN   TENG OK CHOK TSAM KUN TU KHOR WA DUM PO'I NAM PA

light.   All of these pavilions are six feet distant from each other.   They are spherical in appearance,

ཅན།   སྲ་བ་བརྟན་པ་སྲུབ་མེད་པ་རླུང་སེར་བུ་ཙམ་ཡང་མི་ཐར་བ་བར་སྟོང་ཐམས་ཅད

CHEN   SA WA TEN PA SUB MAY PA LUNG SER BU TSAM YANG MI TAR WA BAR TONG TAM

stable, and strong.   They are unbroken and without any gaps.   Not even a little breeze can pass through.

ཨུཏྤལ་སྔོན་པོ་ཁ་བྱེ་མ་ཐག་པས་གང་བར་གྱུར།   ཨི་གེ་བཅུ་པའི་བཟླས་པ་ཅི་ནུས་བྱེད།

CHAY UTPAL NGÖN PO KHA JAY MA TAK PAY GANG WAR GYUR

The empty spaces are filled with newly blossomed blue utpala flowers.   *Recite the ten syllables as much as*

མཐར་འོད་གསལ་དུ་བསྡུ་ཞིང་ཟུང་འཇུག་གི་སྐུར་ལྡང་བ་སྔ་མ་བཞིན་ནོ།   ཡང་ཚེ་སྒྲུབ་ཀྱི་སྐབས་སུ།

possible.   At the end, dissolve into clear light and re-arise into the body of union as set forth previously.   *When doing the long-life*

ༀ༔   ཀྱི་བོའི་འོད་དཔག་མེད་ཀྱི་ཐུགས་རྒྱུད་བསྐུལ་བས་ཕྱག་གི་ལྷུང་བཟེད་ཀྱི་བདུད

CHI WO'I Ö PAK MAY KYI TUK GYU KUL WAY CHAK GI LHUNG ZAY KYI DÜ

practice: Invoking the stream of being of Amitabha on my crown, the nectar of the

རྩི་ཁོལ།   རང་གི་ཀྱི་བོ་ནས་ཞུགས།   ལུས་ཐམས་ཅད་གང་ཞིང་འཆི་མེད་འགྲུབ་པར

TSI KHOL   **RANG GI CHI WO NAY SHUK**   **LU TAM CHAY GANG SHING CHI MAY DRUB PAR**

begging bowl in his hands boils over, enters through my crown, and fills my whole body, accomplishing

གྱུར།   བསམ་ཏེ་ཚེ་སྒྲུབ་སྤེལ་ཚིགས་ཚན་བཟླ་བར་སྐབས་སྐབས་སུ་བྱའོ།   དགེ་བ་འདི་ཡིས

GYUR   *- Thinking in this way, you should recite the long-life mantra sometimes.*   **GE WA DI YI**

deathlessness.   By this virtue may all

སེམས་ཅན་ཀུན།   སྡིག་སྒྲིབ་ཉེས་ལྟུང་ནད་གདོན་ཞི།   ཚེ་དཔལ་བསོད་ནམས་ཡེ

SEM CHEN KUN   **DIK DRIB NYE TUNG NAY DÖN SHI**   **TSE PAL SÖ NAM YE**

sentient beings' wrongdoings, obscurations, faults, downfalls, sickness, and döns be pacified.   May their

ཤེས་རྒྱས།   སྒྲོལ་མའི་གོ་འཕང་མྱུར་ཐོབ་ཤོག   རྒྱལ་མཆོག་ཚེ་དཔག་མེད་པའི

SHE GYE   **DROL MAI GO PANG NYUR TOB SHOK**   **GYAL CHOG TSE PAK MAY PAI**

life, glory, merit, and wisdom increase, and may they swiftly accomplish the realization of Tara.   You are

ཡུམ།   འཆི་མེད་ངེས་པར་སྟེར་བ་མོ།   རིག་པ་འཛིན་མ་བཅོམ་ལྡན་འདས

YUM   **CHI MAY NGE PAR TER WA MO**   **RIK PA DZIN MA CHOM DEN DAY**

the mother of the supreme Victor, Amitayus, the mother who definitely bestows deathlessness.

ཡིད་བཞིན་འཁོར་ལོའི་བཀྲ་ཤིས་ཤོག   ཞེས་སྟེ་བཞི་དགེ་བཅུའི་ཁྲིམས་ཀྱི་ཚོར་འཛིན་དགེ་བར་སྐྱོང

YID SHIN KHOR LO'I TRA SHI SHOK

May there be the auspiciousness of the awareness-holder, the *Bhagavati*, the Wish-Fulfilling Wheel!

བ་བློ་གྲོས་མཚན་ཅན་གྱིས་བུགས་དཁ་ཉམས་བཞེས་ཀྱི་ཆེད་དུ།   སྐོམས་ལས་པ་དྷརྨ་ཀ་རས་འབུ་མཎ་པོའི་ལོ་སྟོན་ཟླ་བོ་

This yidam practice was written at the request of Lodro, King of Dege, who has a wealth of discipline, by the Dharma Kara, the Eighth

དཀར་ཆོས་རྒྱལ་བ་དང་པོ་རྒྱལ་ཕྱར་འགྲུབ་སྟོར་ལ་ལྷུན་གྲུབ་སྟེང་གི་ཕོ་བྲང་ཆེན་པོར་བྲིས་པ་མངྒ་ལོ་ཛ་ཡཎྟུ༎   ༎

Tai Situ,in the year of a rich harvest on an auspicious day during the fortnight of the increasing moon of the eight month, in the great palace of the capital of Lhundrup Teng.   Mangalam dzayentu.

Translated by Karma Sonam Drolma

Appendix B

༄༅། །རྗེ་བཙུན་ཡིད་བཞིན་འཁོར་ལོའི་རྒྱུན་གྱི་རྣལ་འབྱོར་ཁྱེར་བདེ་
འཆི་མེད་གྲུབ་པ་ཞེས་བྱ་བ་བཞུགས་སོ།

An Easy Daily Practice of the Noble Wish-Fulfilling Wheel, Entitled "Accomplishing Deathlessness"

composed by
Jamgön Kongtrul the Great

༄༎ ༀ་སུ་སྟི་སིདྡྷཱ༎ དྲན་པས་བདུད་བཞིའི་འཇིགས་བཅོམ་མ༎ འཆི་མེད་འཕགས་མར་གུས༎

OM SVASTI SIDDHAM   I bow with devotion to the deathless Noble Lady.   Just the thought of her conquers the fears of the

བཏུད་ནས༎ རིང་དུ་འཚོ་སོགས་མཆོག་ཐོབ་ཕྱིར༎ དེ་ཡི་རྒྱུན་ཁྱེར་ཉམས་ལེན་བཤད༎ ཐོ་རངས་སམ་སྟུ་ཐོའི་ཆ་ལ

four maras.   I will explain her daily practice so that the supreme accomplishments of long life and so on can be attained.   At dawn or

བབས་པའི་ཆོ་བདེ་བའི་གདན་ལ་བསམ་གཏན་གྱི་ཆོས་དང་ལྡན་པས་འཁོད་ནས༎ སྒྲོལ་དཀར་རྒྱུན་ཁྱེར་གྱི་བརྒྱུད་པའི

sometime in the early morning, sit down on a comfortable seat in the samadhi posture.   The following is the lineage supplication for the

གསོལ་འདེབས་ནི༎   ན་མོ་གུ་རུ་ཨཱརྻ་ཏཱ་རཱ་ཡེ༎   སྒྲོལ་མ་ངག་གི་དབང་ཕྱུག་གསེར་གླིང་པ༎

daily practice of White Tara: **NAMO GURU ARYA TARA YE**   **DROL MA NGAK GI WANG CHUG SER LING PA**

       NAMO GURU ARYA TARA YE   To Tara, Ngagi Wangchug, and Serlingpa;

ཇོ་བོ་འབྲོམ་སྟོན་སྤྱན་སྔ་སྤྲེ་པའི་ཞབས༎   དྭགས་པོ་དུས་མཁྱེན་རས་ཆེན་སྤོམ་དྲག་པ༎

JOWO DROM TÖN CHEN NGA DRE PAI SHAB   **DAK PO DU KHYEN RAY CHEN POM DRAK PA**

to Lord Atisha, Dromtönpa, Chennga, and Drepa;   to Gampopa, Dusum Khyenpa, [Drogön] Rechen, and

གྲུབ་ཆེན་ཆོས་ཀྱི་བླ་མར་གསོལ་བ་འདེབས༎   ཨོ་རྒྱན་པ་དང་རང་བྱུང་གཡུང་སྟོན་རྒྱལ༎

DRUB CHEN CHÖ KYI LA MAR SOL WA DEB   **ÖR GYEN PA DANG RANG JUNG YUNG TÖN GYAL**

Pomdrakpa;   and to the mahasiddha Karma Pakshi I pray.   At the feet of the victors Orgyenpa, Rangjung

རོལ་རྡོར་མཁའ་སྤྱོད་དབང་པོ་དེ་བཞིན་གཤེགས༎   རིག་རལ་དོན་ལྡན་བན་སྒར

ROL DOR KHA CHÖ WANG PO DE SHIN SHEK   **RIK RAL DÖN DEN BEN GAR**

[Dorje], and Yungtön [Dorje Pal];   Rolpai Dorje, Khachö Wangpo, and Deshin Shekpa;   Rikpai Raldri,

གོ་ཤྲི་རྗེ།   ཆོས་གྲགས་རྒྱ་མཚོའི་ཞབས་ལ་གསོལ་བ་འདེབས།   །སངས་རྒྱས

GO SHRI JAY   **CHÖ DRAK GYAM TSOI SHAB LA SOL WA DEB**   **SANG GYE**

[Tongwa] Dönden, and Bengar [Jampal Zangpo];   Lord Goshri and Chödrak Gyamtso I pray.   To Sangye

མཉན་པ་མི་བསྐྱོད་དཀོན་མཆོག་འབངས།   །དབང་ཕྱུག་རྡོ་རྗེ་ཆོས་དབང་རྣམ་དག་མཚན།

NYEN PA MI CHÖ KÖN CHOG BANG   **WANG CHUG DOR JE CHÖ WANG NAM DAK TSEN**

Nyenpa, Mikyö *[Dorje]* and Könchog Bang;   to Wangchug Dorje, Chökyi Wangchug, and Namdaktsen;

།ཀརྨ་ཆགས་མེད་དུལ་མོ་དཔལ་ཆེན་པོ།   །བསྟན་པའི་ཉིན་མོ་རྗེད་ལ་གསོལ་བ

KAR MA CHAG MAY DUL MO PAL CHEN PO   **TEN PAI NYIN MO JAY LA SOL WA**

to Karma Chagme, Dulmo *[Chöje]*, and Palchenpo *[Chökyi Döndrup];*   and to *[Tai Situ]* Tenpai

འདེབས།   །བདུད་འདུལ་རྡོ་རྗེ་པདྨ་ཉིན་རྗེད་དབང་།   །སྲིད་བཞིའི་གཙུག་རྒྱན་ཐེག

DEB   **DÜ DUL DOR JE PE MA NYIN JAY WANG**   **SI SHI'I TSUK GYEN TEK**

Nyinje I pray.   To Dudul Dorje and Pema Nyinje Wangpo;   to Tekchog Dorje, who is the crown

མཆོག་རྡོ་རྗེ་དང་།   །རྒྱལ་བས་ལུང་བསྟན་ཡོངས་རྫོགས་བསྟན་པའི་བདག   །བློ་གྲོས

CHOG DOR JE DANG   **GYAL WAY LUNG TEN YONG DZOK TEN PAI DAK**   **LO DRÖ**

ornament of samsara and nirvana;   and to you, Lodrö Thaye, Lord of the entire teachings who

མཐའ་ཡས་ཁྱེད་ལ་གསོལ་བ་འདེབས།   །རྡོ་རྗེའི་སྐུ་བརྙེས་མཁའ་ཁྱབ་རྡོ་རྗེ་དང་།

THA YE KHYE LA SOL WA DEB   **DOR JE'I KU NYE KHA KHYAB DOR JE DANG**

was prophesied by the Victor, I pray.   To Khakhyab Dorje, who attained the vajra body;

།པདྨ་དབང་མཆོག་མཁྱེན་བརྩེའི་འོད་ཟེར་རྒྱལ།   །རིགས་ཀུན་ཁྱབ་བདག་རིག་པའི

PE MA WANG CHOG KHYEN TSE'I Ö ZER GYAL   **RIK KUN KHYAB DAK RIK PAI**

to the victors Pema Wangchog *[Gyalpo]* and Khyentse Özer;   and to Rigpe Dorje, pervading lord of all the

༄༅། རྡོ་རྗེ་སོགས། །རྩ་བརྒྱུད་བླ་མ་ཀུན་དངོས་རྗེ་བཙུན་མ། །གང་གི་སྨིན།

DOR JE SOK   TSA GYU LA MA KUN NGÖ JE TSUN MA   GANG GI MIN

families, and the others – To the Noble Lady who embodies all the root and lineage lamas and to those

སྒྲོལ་བཀའ་བབ་བརྒྱུད་པའི་སྲོལ། །རིམ་པ་དྲུག་ལྡན་རྣམས་ལ་གསོལ་བ་འདེབས།

DROL KA BAB GYU PAI SOL   RIM PA DRUK DEN NAM LA SOL WA DEB

who hold the six traditions of her lineage of ripening, liberation, and dispensation I pray.   Bless that I

།བསྐྱེད་སྔགས་རྫོགས་པའི་རིམ་པ་མཐར་ཕྱིན་ཏེ། །འཆི་མེད་ཡེ་ཤེས་རྡོ་རྗེའི་སྐུ་མཆོག

KYE NGAK DZOK PAI RIM PA TAR CHIN TE   CHI MAY YE SHE DOR JE'I KU CHOG

perfect the stages of development, mantra, and completion and accomplish the supreme vajra wisdom

འགྲུབ། །རྒྱལ་བ་ཀུན་བསྐྱེད་ཡིད་བཞིན་འཁོར་ལོ་དང་། །དབྱེར་མེད་དོན

DRUB   GYAL WA KUN KYE YI SHIN KHOR LO DANG   YER MAY DÖN

body of deathlessness.   May I become inseparable from the Wish-Fulfilling Wheel who gives birth to

གཉིས་ལྷུན་གྲུབ་བྱིན་གྱིས་རློབས། སྒྲོལ་དཀར་རྒྱུན་ཁྱེར་གྱི་བརྒྱུད་པའི་གསོལ་བ་འདེབས

NYI LHUN DRUP JIN GYI LAB

all the victors, and spontaneously accomplish the two benefits. *This prayer to the lineage holders of the daily practice*

འདི་བཞིན། དད་དམ་བླ་བྲལ་ཀརྨ་ལྭ་དཔལ་ཕྲགས་བཞིན་ལྷར་ཀརྨ་ངག་དབང་ཡོན་ཏན་རྒྱ་མཚོས་སྦྱིས་བ།

of White Tara was composed by Karma Ngawang Yönten Gyamtso (Jamgön Kongtrul) in response to the request of Karma Lhapal,
one of pure and unexcelled faith.   Mangalam!

མངྒ་ལམ།།   སྐྱབས་སེམས་ནི།   དཀོན་མཆོག་ཀུན་འདུས་བླ་མར་སྐྱབས་སུ་མཆི།

KÖN CHOG KUN DU LA MAR KYAB SU CHI

Now for refuge and generation of bodhicitta: I take refuge in the Lama, the complete embodiment of the

།འགྲོ་ལ་ཕན་ཕྱིར་ཡིད་བཞིན་འཁོར་ལོ་བསྒྲུབ། ཁྱེན་གསུམ། ཚོགས་བསགས་སློ་ན།

DRO LA PEN CHIR YI SHIN KHOR LO DRUB

Three Jewels. I will practice the Wish-Fulfilling Wheel in order to benefit beings. *-Three times.* To gather the

རང་ཉིད་སྒྲོལ་མའི་ཐུགས་སོ་ག་འོད་ཟེར་གྱིས། །འཕགས་མ་ས་ས་བཅས་མདུན་མཁར་སྤྱན།

RANG NYI DROL MAI TUK SOK Ö ZER GYI   **PAK MA SAY CHAY DUN KHAR CHEN**

accumulations, recite as follows: With light rays emanating from my heart center as Tara, I invite the Noble Lady

དྲངས་གྱུར། །བཛྲ་ས་མ་ཛཿ དཀོན་མཆོག་གསུམ་ལ་བདག་སྐྱབས་མཆི།

DRANG GYUR   **BEDZRA SAMADZA**   **KÖN CHOG SUM LA DAK KYAB CHI**

and her sons into the space in front. BEDZRA SAMADZA. I take refuge in the Three Jewels.

སྡིག་པ་མི་དགེ་སོ་སོར་བཤགས། །འགྲོ་བའི་དགེ་ལ་རྗེས་ཡི་རང། །སངས་རྒྱས

DIK PA MI GAY SO SOR SHAK   **DRO WAI GAY LA JAY YI RANG**   **SANG GYE**

I confess each and every sin and unvirtuous action. I rejoice in the virtue of all beings. I hold the

བྱང་ཆུབ་ཡིད་ཀྱིས་བཟུང། །སངས་རྒྱས་ཆོས་དང་ཚོགས་མཆོག་ལ། །བྱང་ཆུབ

JANG CHUB YI KYI ZUNG   **SANG GYE CHÖ DANG TSOK CHOG LA**   **JANG CHUB**

buddhas and bodhisattvas always in my mind. I take refuge in the Buddha, Dharma, and Sangha until

བར་དུ་སྐྱབས་སུ་མཆི། །རང་གཞན་དོན་ནི་རབ་བསྒྲུབ་ཕྱིར། །བྱང་ཆུབ་སེམས་ནི

BAR DU KYAB SU CHI   **RANG SHEN DÖN NI RAB DRUB CHIR**   **JANG CHUB SEM NI**

I attain enlightenment. I give rise to bodhicitta in order to perfectly accomplish the benefit of myself

བསྐྱེད་པར་བགྱི། །བྱང་ཆུབ་མཆོག་གི་སེམས་ནི་བསྐྱེད་བགྱིས་ནས། །སེམས་ཅན

KYE PAR GYI   **JANG CHUB CHOG GI SEM NI KYE GYI NAY**   **SEM CHEN**

and others. Having given rise to the mind of perfect enlightenment, I will care for all sentient beings.

ༀༀ

TAM CHAY DAK GI DRUN DU NYER
I will engage in the supreme and delightful conduct of awakening.

JANG CHUB CHÖ CHOG
May I accomplish

YI ONG CHÖ PAR GYI
buddhahood for the benefit of all beings.

DRO LA PEN CHIR SANG GYE DRUB PAR SHOK
Having thus recited, dissolve the [visualized] assembly and rest in non-

conceptuality.

DRO KUN DAY DEN DUK NGAL GYU CHAY DRAL
May all beings have happiness and be free of suffering and its causes.   May they

DAY DANG MIN DRAL TANG NYOM CHER NAY SHOK
be inseparable from happiness and abide in great impartiality.   *Now the yogas of generation and recitation:*

OM SHUNYATA JNANA BEDZRA SOBHAWA EMAKO HAM
OM SHUNYATA JNANA BEDZRA SOBHAWA EMAKO HAM.

TONG PAI RANG TSAL HUNG GI DRA DANG LAY
The natural power of emptiness manifests

DOR JE'I SUNG KHOR NANG DU CHU SHEL GYI
as the resonant sound of HUNG.   From this arises a vajra protective circle.

SHAL MAY KHANG Ü PAY KAR DA WAI TENG
Within this appears a

TAM LAY UTPAL KAR PO TAM GYI TSEN

Ö TRÖ DÖN NYI JAY DU YONG
watermoon crystal palace, and in its center appear a white lotus and moon disk. On this appears a TAM,
which becomes a white utpala flower marked by the letter TAM.   Light radiates out, accomplishes the two

གྱུར་ལས། །རང་ཉིད་འཕགས་མ་སྒྲོལ་མ་ཟླ་བའི་མདོག །ཞི་འཛུམ་སྒེག་ཉམས་

GYUR LAY RANG NYI PAK MA DROL MA DA WAI DOK SHI DZUM GEK NYAM

benefits, and is reabsorbed. The flower and TAM transform into myself as the Noble Tara, who is the color of the moon. She is peaceful, smiling, beautiful, and radiating light of five colors. Her forehead,

འོད་ཟེར་ལྔ་ལྡན་འཕྲོ། །དཔྲལ་བ་ཕྱག་ཞབས་ཡེ་ཤེས་སྤྱན་བདུན་མཛེས། །ཕྱག་

Ö ZER NGA DEN TRO TRAL WA CHAG SHAB YE SHE CHEN DUN DZAY CHAG

hands, and feet are beautified with seven wisdom eyes. Her right hand is in the gesture of supreme generosity, and the thumb and ring finger of her left hand hold the stem of a white utpala flower at

གཡས་མཆོག་སྦྱིན་གཡོན་པའི་མཐེབ་སྲིན་གྱིས། །ཨུཏྤལ་དཀར་པོའི་སྡོང་བུ་ཐུགས་

YAY CHOG JIN YÖN PAI TEB SIN GYI UTPAL KAR POI DONG BU TUK

her heart. She wears an upper garment of white silk and a lower garment of the five colors.

ཀར་འཛིན། །དར་དཀར་སྟོད་གཡོག་སྣ་ལྔའི་སྨད་དགྲིས་གསོལ། །ནོར་བུ་མུ་

KAR DZIN DAR KAR TÖ YOK NA NGAI MAY TRI SOL NOR BU MU

She is bedecked with beautiful ornaments of jewels, pearls, and lotuses. Her curly hair is bound in

ཏིག་ཆུ་སྐྱེས་མཛེས་རྒྱན་སྤེལ། །དབུ་སྐྲ་ལི་བ་ལྟག་པར་བཅིང་ཞིང་འཕྱུངས། །ཟླ་

TIK CHU KYE DZAY GYEN PEL Ü TRA LI WA TAK PAR CHING SHING CHANG DA

back and hangs freely. She has a moon as her backrest, and is seated in the vajra posture.

བར་རྒྱབ་བརྟེན་རྡོ་རྗེའི་སྐྱིལ་ཀྲུང་བཞུགས། །གནས་གསུམ་ཨོཾ་ཨཱཿཧཱུྃ་གི་འོད་ཟེར་གྱིས།

WAR GYAB TEN DOR JE'I KYIL TRUNG SHUK NAY SUM OM AH HUNG GI Ö ZER GYI

An OM, AH, and HUNG at her three places radiate light, inviting the wisdom deities.

།ཡེ་ཤེས་སེམས་དཔའ་བཛྲ་ས་མ་ཛཿ ཛཿཧཱུྃ་བཾ་ཧོཿ གཉིས་སུ་མེད་པར་ཐིམ། །སླར་

YE SHE SEM PA BEDZRA SAMADZA DZA HUNG BAM HO NYI SU MAY PAR TIM LAR

BEDZRA SAMADZA. DZA HUNG BAM HO. They melt indivisibly into me.

ༀༀ།   །ཡང་འོད་འཕྲོས་རིགས་ལྔ་སྨིན་དྲངས་གྱུར།

YANG Ö TRÖ RIK NGA CHEN DRANG GYUR

Light radiates again, inviting the deities of the five families.

།དབང་ལྷ་རྣམས་ཀྱིས

WANG LHA NAM KYI

"Empowerment deities, please

མངོན་པར་དབང་བསྐུར་སྩོལ།

NGÖN PAR WANG KUR TSOL

grant empowerment."

།གསོལ་བ་བཏབ་པས་དབང་གི་ལྷ་རྣམས་ཀྱིས

SOL WA TAB PAY WANG GI LHA NAM KYI

In response to this prayer, the empowerment deities say,   OM SARWA TATHA

།ཨོཾ་སརྦ་ཏ་ཐཱ་ག་ཏ་ཨ་བྷི་ཀེ་ཀ་ཏ་ས་མ་ཡ་ཤྲི་ཡེ་ཧཱུྃ།

OM SARWA TATHA GATA ABHIKEKATA SAMAYA SHRI YE HUNG

GATA ABHI KEKATA SAMAYA SHRIYE HUNG   and bestow empowerment.

།ཞེས་གསུང་དབང་བསྐུར་སྐུ་གང

SHAY SUNG WANG KUR KU GANG

My body is filled, and

དྲི་མ་དག

DRI MA DAK

stains are purified.

།རིགས་བདག་འོད་དཔག་མེད་ཀྱིས་དབུ་བརྒྱན་གྱུར།

RIK DAK Ö PAK MAY KYI Ü GYEN GYUR

The Lord of the Family, Amitabha, becomes my head ornament.

སྤྲུལ་པའི་ལྷ

TRUL PAI LHA

Emanated

མོས་བདག་ལ་མཆོད་ཅིང་བསྟོད།

MÖ DAK LA CHÖ CHING TÖ

goddesses make offerings and praises to me:

ཨོཾ་ཨཱརྱ་ཏཱ་རེ་བཛྲ་ཨརྒྷཾ་པཱདྱཾ་པུཥྤེ་དྷུ་པེ་ཨཱ་ལོ་ཀེ་ག་ནྡྷེ

OM ARYA TARE BEDZRA ARGHAM, PADYAM, PUKPE, DUPE, ALOKE,

OM ARYA TARE BEDZRA ARGHAM, PADYAM, PUKPE, DUPE,

ནེ་ཝི་དེ་ཤབྡ་པྲ་ཏི་ཙྪ་ཨཱཿཧཱུྃ་སྭཱ་ཧཱ

GENDHE, NEWIDE, SHABDA PRATITSA AH HUNG SOHA

ALOKE, GENDHE, NEWIDE, SHABDA PRATITSA AH HUNG SOHA.

།ལྷ་དང་ལྷ་མིན་ཅོད་པན་གྱིས

LHA DANG LHA MIN CHÖ PEN GYI

"We pay homage to and praise the mother

།ཞབས་ཀྱི

SHAB

པདྨོ་ལ་བཏུད་དེ།

KYI PE MO LA TÜ DE

།ཕོངས་པ་ཀུན་ལས་སྒྲོལ་མཛད་མ།

PONG PA KUN LAY DROL DZAY MA

སྒྲོལ་མ་ཡུམ་ལ

DROL MA YUM LA

Tara, who liberates from all misfortune, and to whose lotus feet even the devas and asuras bow with their

ཕྱག་འཚལ་བསྟོད།   ཅེས་པས་བསྟོད།   ཐུགས་ཀར་པད་ཟླར་འཁོར་ལོའི་ལྟེ་བར་ཏཱཾ།

CHAG TSAL TÖ   **TUK KAR PAY DAR KHOR LOI TAY WAR TAM**

crowns." - *Thus praising.*   In my heart on a lotus and moon is a wheel.   In its center is a TAM.   Above

སྟེང་འོག་ཨོཾ་ཧ་རྩིབས་བརྒྱད་ཡིག་འབྲུ་བརྒྱད།   གཡས་བསྐོར་སྟོན་ཟླའི་མདོག་ཅན།

TENG OK OM HA TSIB GYE YIG DRU GYE   **YAY KOR TÖN DAI DOK CHEN YO**

the TAM is an OM and below it is a HA.   On the eight spokes are the eight *[remaining]* syllables facing

གཡོ་མེད་གསལ།   ཨོཾ་ཏཱ་རེ་ཏུཏྟཱ་རེ་ཏུ་རེ་སྭཱ་ཧཱ།   ཞེས་རྩ་སྔགས་ལ་བཟླས་པའི་དངོས།

MAY SAL   **OM TARE TUTTARE TURE SOHA**

inward.   They are bright and clear, the color of the autumn moon.   OM TARE TUTTARE TURE SOHA

གཞི་བྱ།   ཚེ་ཞེས་ཅན་བཟླ་བའི་ཚེ།   ཏཱཾ་མཐར་ཨོཾ་ཧའི་བར་དུ་ཕྲིལ་སྔགས།

Thus do the main practice, which is the recitation of the root mantra.
When you wish to do the long-life supplement, [recite as follows]:   **TAM TAR OM HA'I BAR DU PEL NGAK**

Around the TAM *[on the hub of the wheel]*

འཁོད།   འོད་འཕྲོས་རང་གཞན་སྒྲིབ་སྦྱངས་ཚེ་དཔལ་སྤེལ།   འཕགས་མཆོད།

KHÖ   **Ö TRÖ RANG SHEN DRIB JANG TSE PAL PEL**   **PAK CHÖ**

is the long-life mantra between the OM and the HA.   It radiates light, purifying the obscurations of myself
and others and increasing our life spans and brilliance.   Making offerings to the noble ones, it collects

བྱིན་རླབས་བརྟན་གཡོའི་ཚེ་བཅུད་བསྡུས།   རང་ཐིམ་ཚེ་དང་ཡེ་ཤེས་མཆོག

JIN LAB TEN YO'I TSE CHU DU   **RANG TIM TSE DANG YE SHE CHOG**

their blessings, as well as the life essences of the inanimate and animate.   Melting back into me, I attain

ཐོབ་གྱུར།   ཨོཾ་ཏཱ་རེ་ཏུཏྟཱ་རེ་ཏུ་རེ་མ་མ་ཨཱ་ཡུཿཔུ་ཎྱེ་ཛྙཱ་ན་པུཥྚིཾ་ཀུ་རུ་སྭཱ་ཧཱ།

TOB GYUR   **OM TARE TUTTARE TURE MAMA AYU PUNYE JNANA PUKTRIM KURU SOHA**

supreme life and wisdom.   OM TARE TUTTARE TURE MAMA AYU PUNYE JNANA PUKTRIM KURU SO HA.

༄༅། ཚེ་སྒྲུབ་དང་རྒྱུན་གྱི་རྣལ་འབྱོར་ལ་འདི་གཙོ་བོར་བཟླ། སྐབས་སུ། རི་གས་

During long-life practice and regular daily practice
this is the main recitation.   Sometimes recite the following: "Lama, Lord of the Family, please grant deathlessness

RIK

བདག་ལ་བླ་མས་འཆི་མེད་ཚེ་དབང་སྩོལ། ཁྱེད་པས་རྒྱུད་བསྐུལ་དེ་ཡི་ཐུགས་འོད་ཀྱིས།

DAK LA MAY CHI MAY TSE WANG TSOL   **GU PAY GYU KUL DAY YI TUK Ö KYI**

and the power of life."   Through my devotion his stream of being is invoked.   Light from his heart gathers

འཁོར་འདས་བརྟན་གཡོའི་ཚེ་བཅུད་དྭངས་མ་བསྡུས། ལྷུང་བཟེད་ནང་ཞུགས་ཤུ་ཁོལ།

KHOR DAY TEN YO'I TSE CHU DANG MA DU   **LHUNG ZAY NANG SHUK SHU KHOL**

in the vital essence and energy of the inanimate and animate in samsara and nirvana, which enters into his

ཁ་ནས་ལུད། རང་ལུས་འཆི་མེད་བདུད་རྩིས་གང་བར་གྱུར། ཞེས་མོས་ལ།

KHA NAY LU   **RANG LU CHI MAY DÜ TSI GANG WAR GYUR**

begging bowl.   Melting, it boils and overflows.   My body becomes filled with deathless dutsi.   - *Visualizing*

ཨོཾ་ཏཱ་རེ་ཏུཏྟཱ་རེ་ཏུ་རེ་མ་མ་ཨཱ་ཡུཿ་པུཎྱེ་ཛྙཱ་ན་པུཥྚི་ཾ་ཀུ་རུ་སྭཱ་ཧཱ། ཞེས་བཟླའོ།

OM TARE TUTTARE TURE MAMA AYU PUNYE JNANA PUKTRIM KURU SOHA

that, recite: OM TARE TUTTARE TURE MAMA AYU PUNYE JNANA PUKTRIM KURU SOHA.   *At the*

ཕུན་མཐར་བསྡུ་ལྡང་ནི། སྣོད་བཅུད་འོད་ཞུ་ཏཾ་དང་བདག་ཉིད་ཀྱང། མི་དམིགས་འོད།

end of the session, the dissolution   **NÖ CHU Ö SHU TAM DANG DAK NYI KYANG**   **MI MIK Ö**

and re-arisal are as follows: The vessel *[the outer world]* and its contents melt into light.   Then I and the TAM

གསལ་ཆག་རྒྱ་ཆེན་མོར་ཐིམ། ཿ ལར་ཡང་འཕགས་མའི་སྐུར

SAL CHAG GYA CHEN MOR TIM   **LAR YANG PAK MAI KUR**

merge into nonconceptual clear light, mahamudra.   ***   I reappear clearly in the form of the Noble

གསལ་འབྲུ་གསུམ་མཆན།   ཆོས་ཀུན་ལྷ་སྔགས་ཡེ་ཤེས་རོལ་པའོ།

SAL DRU SUM TSEN   **CHÖ KUN LHA NGAK YE SHE ROL PA'O**

Lady, adorned with the three syllables.   All phenomena are the play of the deity, mantra, and wisdom.

གཏོར་འབུལ་སློ།   རཾ་ཡཾ་ཁཾ།   རིན་ཆེན་སྣོད་དུ་འབྲུ་གསུམ་འོད་དུ་ཞུ།

RAM YAM KHAM   **RIN CHEN NÖ DU DRU SUM Ö DU SHU**

If you wish to offer torma, recite as follows: RAM YAM KHAM   Within a precious vessel, the three seed

གཏོར་མ་ཟག་མེད་བདུད་རྩིའི་རྒྱ་མཚོར་གྱུར།   ཨོཾ་ཨཱཿཧཱུྃ།   ལན་གསུམ།

TOR MA ZAG MAY DÜ TSI GYAM TSOR GYUR   **OM AH HUNG**

syllables melt into light.   They become a torma, an ocean of undefiled dutsi.   OM AH HUNG   *- **Three times.***

ཐུགས་སྲོག་འོད་ཀྱིས་སྲས་བཅས་རྗེ་བཙུན་མ།   མདུན་མཁར་ཆེན་དྲངས།

TUK SOK Ö KYI SAY CHAY JE TSUN MA   **DUN KHAR CHEN DRANG**

Light rays from the center of my heart invite the Noble Lady and her sons into the space in front.

བཛྲ་ས་མཱ་ཛཿ   པདྨ་ཀ་མ་ལ་ཡ་སྟྭཾ།   ཨོཾ་ཏཱ་རེ་ཏུ་ཏྟཱ་རེ་ས་པ་རི་ཝཱ་ར་ཨི་དྃ་བ

BEDZRA SAMADZA   **PEMA KAMALA YA SA TAM**   **OM TARE TUTTARE SAPARI WARA**

BEDZRA SAMADZA   PEMA KAMALA YA SA TAM   OM TARE TUTTARE SAPARIWARA

ལིང་ཏ་ཁ་ཁ་ཁཱ་ཧི་ཁཱ་ཧི།   ལན་གསུམ་གྱིས་ཕུལ།   ཨོཾ་ཨཱརྱ་ཏཱ་རེ་བཛྲ་ཨརྒྷཾ་པཱདྱཾ་པུཥྤེ

IDAM BALINGTA KAKA KAHI KAHI   **OM ARYA TARE BEDZRA ARGHAM, PADYAM,**

IDAM BALINGTA KAKA KAHI KAHI   *- Offer with **three repetitions.***   OM ARYA TARE BEDZRA ARGHAM, PADYAM,

 དྷཱུ་པེ་ཨཱ་ལོ་ཀེ་གནྡྷེ་ནཻ་ཝི་དྱ་ཤབྡ་པྲ་ཏཱི་ཙྪ་ཨཱཿཧཱུྃ་སྭཱ་ཧཱ།   གྱིས་མཆོད།

PUKPE, DHUPE, ALOKE, GENDHE, NEWIDE, SHABDA PRATITSA AH HUNG SOHA

PUKPE, DHUPE, ALOKE, GENDHE, NEWIDE, SHABDA PRATITSA AH HUNG SOHA   *- Thus make the offerings.*

ༀༀ། །འཁོར་བ་ལས་སྒྲོལ་ཏ་རེ་མ། ྅ྲཏ་ཏཱ་རེ་ཡིས་འཇིགས་བརྒྱད་སྒྲོལ།

KHOR WA LAY DROL TA RE MA   **TU TA RE YI JIK GYE DROL**

You are the mother, TARE, who liberates from samsara.   With TUTTARE you free us from the eight

ཏུ་རེས་ནད་རྣམས་ལས་སྒྲོལ། སྒྲོལ་མ་ལ་ཡང་ཕྱག་འཚལ་བསྟོད། ཅེས་པས་བསྟོད།

TU RE NA WA NAM LAY DROL   **DROL MA LA YANG CHAG TSAL TÖ**

dangers.   With TURE you protect from all illness.   I praise and bow to the mother, who liberates.   - *Thus*

འཕགས་མ་རྒྱལ་བ་སྲས་བཅས་ཀྱིས། མཆོད་གཏོར་བཞེས་ལ་བདག་འཁོར་བཅས།

PAK MA GYAL WA SAY CHAY KYI   **CHÖ TOR SHE LA DAK KHOR CHAY**

make the praises.   Noble Lady, Victors, and your sons!   Having accepted this offering torma, please grant me

རྟག་ཏུ་སྲུངས་སྐྱོབས་བྱིན་གྱིས་རློབས། ཆོས་སྤྱོད་ཡུན་རིང་འཚོ་བ་དང་།

TAK TU SUNG KYOB JIN GYI LOB   **CHÖ CHÖ YUN RING TSO WA DANG**

and those connected to me your blessings, and continually protect and guard us.   Please sustain Dharma

མཆོག་མཐུན་དངོས་གྲུབ་མ་ལུས་སྩོལ། ཞིག་བརྒྱས་ཆོངས་པ་བཤགས། རྟེན་མེད་ན

CHOG TUN NGÖ DRUB MA LU TSOL

activity for a very long time, and grant us all the ordinary and supreme siddhis without exception.   *With the*

བཛྲ་མུཿ ག་ཞིགས། ཨོད་ག ༀ་སུ་ཏྲ་ཏིཀྟ་བཛྲ་ཡ་སྭཱ་ཧཱ་བཅན

BEDZRA MU   **OM SUTRA TIKTA BEDZRA YA SO HA**

100-syllable mantra, confess all errors.   *If you have no representation, [the deities] depart with* BEDZRA MU.   *If you have one,*

བཤགས་གྲ དགེ་འདིས་རྒྱལ་ཡུམ་ཤེས་རབ་པ་རོལ་ཕྱིན། བདག་གཞན

GAY DI GYAL YUM SHE RAB PA ROL CHIN   **DAK SHEN**

invite the deities to remain there with OM SUTRA TIKTA BEDZRA YA SOHA   By this virtue, may I and all other

འགྲོ་བ་ཀུན་གྱིས་མྱུར་འགྲུབ་ཅིང༌།   ཚེ་ཀུན་རྗེ་བཙུན་སྒྲོལ་མས་རྗེས་སུ་བཟུང༌།

DRO WA KUN GYI NYUR DRUB CHING   **CHAY KUN JE TSUN DROL MAY JAY SU ZUNG**

beings quickly attain the state of the mother of the Victors, Prajnaparamita.   In all our lives, may the

ཚེ་དང་ཡེ་ཤེས་རྒྱས་པའི་བཀྲ་ཤིས་ཤོག   ཅེས་བསྔོ་སྨོན་དང་བཀྲ་ཤིས་ཀྱིས

TSE DANG YE SHE GYE PAI TRA SHI SHOK

venerable Tara care for us with her compassion.   May there be the auspicious flowering of long life and

wisdom.   *Through these prayers of dedication, aspiration, and auspiciousness, may there be good fortune!*

དགེ་ལེགས་སུ་གྱུར༌   ལྷག་པའི་ལྷ་མཆོག་ཀུན་ལས་ཀྱང༌།   བྱིན་རླབས་མྱུར་ཞིང་ཆེ༌

LHAK PAI LHA CHOG KUN LAY KYANG   **JIN LAB NYUR SHING TSE**

She is the one who increases life.   Her blessings are even more swift than those of all the most exalted

དཔེ་ལ་མ༌   ཇོ་བོ་ལུགས་བཞིན་སྒྲུབ་པའི་ཐབས༌   འདིར་འབྲེལ་ཀུན་གྱི་མཆོག

PEL MA   **JO WO LUK SHIN DRUB PAI TAB**   **DIR DREL KUN GYI CHOG**

deities.   May anyone who is connected with this practice, which is in the tradition of Lord Atisha,

འགྲུབ་ཤོག   འཕགས་མ་སྒྲུབ་པའི་རྒྱུན་ཁྱེར་འདིའང་རིག་འཛིན་ཌཱ་ཀྱི་པདྨ་ཚེ་དབང་དཔལ་མོས་བཀྲ

DRUB SHOK

attain the supreme accomplishment!   *This daily practice of the Noble Lady was composed by Lodrö Thaye in*

ཤིས་པའི་ལྷ་རྫས་བཅས་བསྐུལ་བོར་བློ་གྲོས་མཐའ་ཡས་ཀྱིས་ཚེ་འཕེལ་ཟླ་བའི་དཀར་ཕྱོགས་ཀྱི་དགའ་བ་གཉིས་པ་འགྲུབ

response to a request and offerings of auspicious divine substances by the awareness holder and dakini Pema Tsewang Palmo.

པའི་སྐྱོར་བ་དང་ལྡན་པའི་དུས་བཟང་པོར་དེ་བྱི་ཀོ་ཊི་སྟེ་སྙིང་པོ་རྟག་བརྟན་དགའ་ཚལ་དུ་སྤེལ་བ་དགེ་ལེགས་འཕེལ༎

It was composed at an excellent time during the second "Joy" of the waxing moon during the month of miracles at Devikoti in Nyingpo
Takten Gatsal. May it spread, and may virtue and goodness increase!

Translated by Karma Sonam Drolma

Appendix C

རིང་འཚོའི་བདེན་ཚིག་བཏུགས་སོ།

"True Words of Longevity"

(Long-Life Prayer for the Venerable Khenpo Karthar Rinpoche)

composed by

The Seventeenth Gyalwa Karmapa
Ogyen Trinley Palden Wangi Dorje

ༀ།   །བསྐལ་པ་མང་པོར་རང་གོམས་ཚོགས་གཉིས་ལམ།   །མཐར་ཕྱིན་འབྲས།

KAL PA MANG POR RANG GOM TSOK NYI LAM   **TAR CHIN DRAY**

Having completed the path of the two accumulations during many kalpas, you have

བུའི་ཆོས་སྐུར་གནས་གྱུར་ཅིང་།   །མཉམ་མེད་ཡོན་ཏན་མཐའ་ཡས་རྣད་བྱུང་དཔལ།

BU'I CHÖ KUR NAY GYUR CHING   **NYAM ME YÖN TEN TA YEH MAY JUNG PAL**

been transformed into its result, the dharmakaya.   Boundless splendor of peerless qualities – Victors of the

།དུས་གསུམ་རྒྱལ་བ་རྣམས་ཀྱིས་དགེ་ལེགས་སྩོལ།   །བཅོས་མིན་དད་པས་བླ་མའི་བཀའ

DU SUM GYAL WA NAM KYI GE LEK TSOL   **CHÖ MIN DE PAY LA MAI KA**

three times, bestow virtue and excellence.   With uncontrived faith you listen to the guru's words as

ལྟར་མཉན།   །ལུང་རིག་བདུད་ཅིས་ཐུགས་ཀྱི་བུམ་བཟང་གཏམས།   །བ་ཤད་སྒྲུབ

TAR NYEN   **LUNG RIK DÜ TSI TUK KYI BUM ZANG TAM**   **SHAY DRUB**

commands.   The good vase of your heart is filled with the ambrosia of scripture and reason.   Your

ལས་ལ་རྟག་གུས་བཙོན་པས་ཞུགས།   །རྒྱལ་བསྟན་འདེགས་པའི་དམ་པ་ཞབས་བརྟན

LAY LA TAK GU TSÖN PAY SHUK   **GYAL TEN DEK PAI DAM PA SHAB TEN**

exertion in teaching and practice is continuous and devoted.   May the lotus feet of this genuine upholder

གསོལ།   །སྔོན་མེད་ཡུལ་དུ་ཆོས་ཀྱི་སྒྲོན་མེ་སྤར   །རིས་མེད་འགྲོ་ལ་སེམས་ཀྱི་བདེ

SOL   **NGÖN ME YUL DU CHÖ KYI DRÖN ME PAR**   **RI ME DRO LA SEM KYI DE**

of the Victor's doctrine remain firm.   You light the torch of dharma in a country where it did not exist.   You

སྐྱེད་བསྐྲུན།   །འཚོ་མེད་ཞི་བདེའི་ལམ་ལ་རྟག་པར་གནས།   །སྐྱོན་མེད་ཁྲིམས་ལྡན

KYI TRUN   **TSE ME SHI DE'I LAM LA TAK PAR NAY**   **KYÖN ME TRIM DEN**

impartially give rise to happiness in the minds of beings.   You always remain on the path of harmless peace

དམ་པ་ཞབས་བརྟན་གསོལ།   ཀྲམ་དག་དགེ་བའི་ལྷག་བསམ་དྲི་མེད་དང་།   ཁྲུ་

DAM PA SHAB TEN SOL   **NAM DAK GE WA'I LHAK SAM DRI ME DANG**   **LU**

and joy.   May the feet of this flawless genuine monk remain firm.   Through stainless altruistic pure virtue,

མེད་སྨོན་ལམ་བཟང་དང་མཐུ་བཙན་པོས།   འདོད་པའི་འབྲས་བཟང་མྱུར་དུ་རྫོགས་དང་

ME MÖN LAM ZANG DANG TU TSEN PÖ   **DÖ PAI DRAY ZANG NYUR DU DZOK DANG**

and through the power of unfailing good aspirations, may the good result we wish for be quickly attained,

ལྷན།   ཀུན་ལ་སྣང་བ་དཀར་པོས་ཁྱབ་གྱུར་ཅིག   ཅེས་པ་མཁན་གར་མཐར་རིན་པོ་ཆེའི་

LHEN   **KUN LA NANG WA KAR PÖ KHAB GYUR CHIK**

and may all be filled with the radiance of virtue.   *In response to the earnest request of Khenpo Karthar*

ཞབས་བརྟན་འདི་བཞིན་ཉིད་ཀྱི་སློབ་ཚོགས་རྣམས་ཀྱིས་བསྐུལ་མ་ནན་ཆེར་བྱུང་དོན་བཞིན་གཡུ་སྒྲུབ་པའི་མཚན་འཛིན་ཨོ་རྒྱན་

Rinpoche's disciples for a longevity supplication like this, this was written immediately at Gyuto Monastery in India on

ཕྲིན་ལས་དཔལ་ལྡན་དབང་གི་རྡོ་རྗེས་ཕྱི་ལོ་༢༠༠༢ཕྱི་ཟླ་༥ཚེས་༦ལ་འཕགས་ཡུལ་རྒྱུད་སྟོད་གྲྭ་ཚང་དུ་ཡར་མར་བྲིས་པ་ལུ་སྟེ།

May 6th, 2002, by Ogyen Trinley Palden Wangi Dorje, who bears the name Karmapa.

Translation © Yeshe Gyamtso.

Appendix D

A Chronology of the Direct Lineage of the Karma Kagyu for the White Tara Practice

A Chronology of the Direct Lineage of the Karma Kagyu for the White Tara Practice

956–1040	Ngagi Wangchug (*Vagishvarakirti*)
?	Serlingpa (*Suvarnadvipi*)
982–1054	Lord Atisha (*Atisha Dipamkara*)
1005–1064	Dromtönpa
1038–1103	Chennga Tsultrim Bar
?	Yepay Drepa
1079–1159	Gampopa (*Dhakpo Lhaje*)
1110–1193	Dusum Khyenpa (*the first Karmapa*)
1088–1158	Drogön Rechenpa (*an earlier life of the first Tai Situ*)
?	Pomdrakpa
1206–1283	Karma Pakshi (*the mahasiddha Chökyi Lama, the second Karmapa*)
1230–1309	Orgyenpa
1284–1339	Rangjung Dorje (*the third Karmapa*)
1284–1365	Yungtön Dorje Pal (*Yungtön Shikpo*)
1340–1383	Rolpe Dorje (*the fourth Karmapa*)
1350–1405	Khachö Wangpo (*the second Shamarpa*)
1384–1415	Deshin Shekpa (*the fifth Karmapa*)
?	Rigpe Raldri (*Pandita Sowon Kashipa*)
1416–1453	Tongwa Dönden (*the sixth Karmapa*)
?	Bengar Jampal Zangpo
1427–1489	Lord Goshri (*the first Gyaltsap Rinpoche*)
1454–1506	Chödrak Gyamtso (*the seventh Karmapa*)
?	Sangye Nyenpa (*the siddha Tashi Paljor*)
1507–1554	Mikyö Dorje (*the eighth Karmapa*)
1525–1583	Könchog Bang (*Könchok Yenlak, the fifth Shamarpa*)
1556–1603	Wangchug Dorje (*the ninth Karmapa*)
1584–1630	Chökyi Wangchug (*the sixth Shamarpa*)
?	Namdaktsen (*Karma Namdak*)
1613–1678	Karma Chagme
?	Dulmo Chöje
1659–1732	Palchenpo Chökyi Döndrup (*the eighth Shamarpa*)
1700–1774	Tenpai Nyinje (*the eighth Tai Situ*)
1733–1797	Dudul Dorje (*the thirteenth Karmapa*)
1774–1853	Pema Nyinje Wangpo (*the ninth Tai Situ*)
1798–1868	Tekchog Dorje (*the fourteenth Karmapa*)
1813–1899	Lodrö Thaye (*the first Jamgön Kongtrul*)
1871–1922	Khakhyab Dorje (*the fifteenth Karmapa*)
1886–1952	Pema Wangchog Gyalpo (*the eleventh Tai Situ*)
1904–1953	Khyentse Özer (*one of the five "second Kongtruls"*)
1924–1981	Rigpe Dorje (*the sixteenth Karmapa*)